THROUGH THE STORM

A Polio Story

Through the Storm
A Polio Story

Robert F. Hall

NORTH STAR PRESS OF ST. CLOUD, INC.

*Dedicated to my four children
Chris, Betsy, Mark and Deborah
with love*

Library of Congress Cataloging-in-Publication Data

Hall, Robert F. 1926-
    Through the storm : a polio story / Robert F. Hall.
    160 p. 21.5 cm.
    ISBN 0-87839-059-6 : $12.95
    1. Hall, Robert F. 1926---Health. 2. Poliomyelitis--Patients-
-United States--Biography. I. Title.
    RC181.U5H35   1990
    362.1'96835'0092--dc20
[B]
                      90-36783
                      CIP

Cover photo, "Thunderstorm clouds north of Johnstown" courtesy of the Nebraska Game and Parks Commission.

ISBN: 0-87839-059-6

Published by:
North Star Press of St. Cloud, Inc.
P.O. Box 451
St. Cloud, Minnesota 56302

FOREWORD

My secretary, Ann Zellmer, gave me a glass paperweight with a prophetic message etched on the clear glass: "What you dare to dream, dare to do!" Next, a letter from my friend, Judy Lane, said in part, "you write well." Those two contemporary events, colliding somewhat like a hot and cold front, spawned a creative wind which blew such a gale, my writing was launched. *Through the Storm* billowed up in my mind and became a reality on paper. I was receptive to this creative energy, but I could not have predicted the stormy outcome when two friends edited my first text.

Jack Goodwin and Gloria Benson must have been very good friends of mine, because they still are after their editing. I don't know whether they were more kind than blunt, but they were both. And, they were basic. "You can't write it like that," was one notation. But I survived the deluge.

Uplifted by this new text of high pressure editing, I soon became puzzled by the shower of rejection slips from prospective publishers. A friend from my support group hailed Brad Ayers for me, who, for a price, taught me how to make my book presentable to publishers in prospectus form. But a strong head wind of increasing rejection slips fashioned a stationary front for finding publication. I was receiving more rejection slips quicker with my streamlined presentation.

I turned to other friends for help in storming the publishing game (I own over one hundred rejection slips). Erv and Marjorie Kreidberg, George Dixon, Jack Barnhart, Dr. J. Kent Canine of Sister Kenny Institute, and Joan Headley of the International Polio Network, were all helpful and essential in bringing my book to publication. Two midwives, Judy Lane and Corinne Dwyer, squeezed me to cut the text, cut again, and then there was birth. And I was left with enough material for a second book as to how we all coped after polio. To all who helped me, my sincere thanks.

Author's Note

The medical description of polio in this book is written at the lay level and is not professional or scientific as we understand polio today. However, polio is represented as it was understood in the mainstream of our society during those epidemic years. Even then, among professionals, there was a wide variety of opinions as to how many kinds of polio there were, how polio was transmitted and how it was to be treated. A very large part of the fear connected with polio was what we did not know about it.

Bob Hall

CONTENTS

THROUGH THE STORM

A Polio Story

PART I
The Storm

CHAPTER ONE

The Big Chill

Polio is spectacular, the way it strikes, the way it kills, the way it leaves its trademark. It hits like a fierce Nebraska straight-line storm in the heat of summer, suddenly smashing and destroying all before it with cold fury.

It is most spectacular during its initial blasts, when it pelts down entire families with agony, or flashes an individual with a wrenching, lightning-like strike. Polio sears an arm or a leg with withering results. It hurts body and soul; numbs the heart. No one is safe. There is no storm cellar that can offer protection against it. Polio storms in so completely on humanity that active fallout can be measured only at the dangerously high level of paralyzing fear. Total pervasive fear.

Eventually, out of this chaos emerges the single lesson of patience—patience absolutely essential for the restoration of the whole person to health. For, as the polio storm subsides, and the rising barometer reveals a higher fear build-up, patience must be practiced diligently and carefully if there is life to be lived beyond fear. In my story, blue sky, calm, with a few light breezes, becomes the revised forecast for the survivors.

My polio started out innocently enough. At first, I thought, "It's just another case of sinus."

During the Dust Bowl years, I had experienced many sinus attacks and was frequently hospitalized as a youngster with sinus infections. That was before either sulfa or penicillin was available to stem the infection. Now older, perhaps I was mistaken to think I had outgrown that illness.

1

By the middle of the summer of 1949, I was still run down from all that was involved in graduating from Yale. The final exams weren't so bad, but the comprehensive examinations in my undergraduate history major required exhaustive preparation. This included reviewing studies I had completed before serving in the army. Then, the last gasp in getting my thesis typed and printed, and just plain burning the candle at both ends saying "good-bye" to my friends left me drained. Yale asked a great deal from a person to graduate, and in addition to all that, I had to finish my college bursary research job so I could pay my final bills to the university if I wanted to graduate.

Then moving back to Omaha to live in my aunt and uncle's home was a major change for me, to say nothing of getting my first job at the stock yards. Working at that job meant I had to rise early to catch the 5:10 a.m. bus to work. Although it was then well into the summer, my complexion remained tattletale gray. My stamina registered about the same gray quality from my earlier graduation fatigue. But somehow, all the grayness seemed appropriate to mark my early morning rising for work.

There was a touch of irony to this new life of employment I had chosen. During my last year at college, I had become active in the labor management club and was involved in labor management decisions. I believed work in this area represented a new and exciting frontier in our society.

It had been during this last year at Yale that an imposing history professor had challenged our class. He provided perspective to our setting and painted in some great opportunities for our imaginations to feast on. I was excited about what I heard was out there in our emerging post-war expanding economy. I was eager to make some of my dreams come true.

I had no thoughts about disease or physical disability. They were not my concern. The polio epidemic was far removed from me. The crippling disease was something I read about in the newspapers. I had no feelings for it. For who could have foreseen that after my splendid year at Yale was over, and just after I had returned to Nebraska to take my first job in pursuit of my dreams, that my world would be turned upside down? That my dreams would become a nightmare in a terrible storm?

The weekend before I became ill, I went swimming with my friends in a sand pit. That involved much underwater tag in the cold clear water. We swam around some pilings of an old abandoned dredge, and some of us went down deep to hide in the darker colder water. I went deeper than anyone else. It cooled me from the searing heat for a while. The cooling didn't last long. After tennis on Monday, my appetite went downhill through the rest of the week. It became harder and harder for me to catch that 5:10 a.m. bus to Swift and Company.

At the plant, I was working as a standards checker in the third subbasement, checking the time and motion effectiveness of the union workers carting hams and briskets to the sweet pickle department. The workers didn't exactly relish my checking out their work efficiency.

Several times a day, I had to shed my long white working coat that kept me warm in the clammy 42-degree atmosphere in that subbasement. I trudged up the three flights of stairs to the ground floor to take some pertinent information over to the main office building. Outside, we were having our usual late July Nebraska summer of 90 to 100 degrees. On the Friday that I became ill in that clammy subbasement, I climbed the stairs to go outside into 104 degrees. When I went outside into that searing heat, it felt as if someone was hitting me over the head with a sledge hammer. A coworker was kind enough to drive me home as I became miserable with high fever accompanied by violent chills and a fierce headache.

"Another case of sinus," I thought to myself. "I've been really stupid, not taking care of myself. Underwater swimming is always hard on the sinuses, and I did go way down deep several times. And now, I'm probably going to miss Nancy's wedding here at the house next weekend. Maybe even have to go to the hospital again."

Back at the house, my nose and throat doctor made a house call and told me I was not having a sinus attack. "Well, flu then" was my next thought. "But I should have been more careful."

"It could be the flu," was his reply, and then he reached up to pull my head forward slightly. That was when I first noticed that my back was sore and my neck stiff. The muscles in my legs were tender to his touch. He was a young assistant to my regular ENT doctor and I was aware that he was anxious to be on his way from his house call. He suggested that I call my family physician as he left. I looked up at my uncle at the doorway, and I could see both of us were beginning to think of the same thing. Polio!

In the evening, my uncle drove me to the hospital for observation. My physician, an old family friend, said he couldn't be sure what I had. Since he could not account for the high fever and headache, he wanted a closer look at me. I told him about the deep muscle spasms that I had first noticed late in the afternoon. "They are quivering spasms which seem to take hold of my entire leg. They are like mice running inside my muscles from the thigh all the way to the ankle."

But I laughed at trying to make a connection between those spasms with my headache and fever.

By then, I was beginning to have serious thoughts about polio. Of course I didn't know a thing about it except that if you got it some awful things could happen. It killed quite a few people, and it disabled a lot more in some awful ways. Arms and legs shriveled up. I didn't want to dwell on it too much. My doctor frankly told me that it could be polio, but he wasn't sure. At night my neck grew stiffer, and I had one of the nurses rub it, which made me feel better. I remember thinking, "She is a real pretty girl, worth looking up when I get out of the hospital."

She was the last nurse I thought about in that way for a long time. The next morning, I was going to have my spine tapped. It was scary. My physician explained the procedure: "I'm going to extract some fluid from your spinal cord. The tap will be in your lower back. I want you to double up as much as possible so the vertebrae in your back will be spread apart to allow the needle to pass easily into the spinal cord. The fluid will tell us if you have polio. The tap should not hurt much, but you may have a headache afterwards. The prick of the novocain is apt to hurt much more than the tap itself."

His description proved to be accurate, because he knew what he was doing, and he had a true hand. I was able to double up quite well so the vertebrae did spread. The substantial needle drew off the spinal fluid. No headache followed. This was the first of seven spinal taps I received.

In the fluid which the doctor extracted from my spinal cord, there was supposed to be a clear message. Either I did, or did not, have polio. The cell count and the protein count could not be mistaken. The answer was not long in coming. In just a short time, a nurse came to the door of my room and closed it. She did so without saying a word. That is how I learned I had polio. I felt very much alone. I was probably scared, but it was too early for me to tell.

CHAPTER TWO

Hot Packs and Enemas

There was only one hospital in our city with a polio ward and I had to be transferred to it by ambulance. County Hospital was a large yellow brick building with receding decks built in the 1930s. Entering there was good-bye to the outside world for a while and the take-off into the unknown. Something besides my polio was working up my back, and by the time it reached my neck, I recognized what it was. It was fear. Where I was going, anything could happen. Anything! Many situations ran through my mind. It was a wonder I could rationalize a sane point of view with the visions I cooked up for myself. "What would I do if—?"

Coming onto the long gray isolation ward on the west side of the building, I was introduced to a few ward mates ranging in age from 12 to 49. I found myself placed in a stall that had a glass partition reaching up a couple of feet. I wondered if that was what it felt like to go to prison, but I still wanted to trust the nurses and doctors.

My bed, fitted alternately across with strips of cotton and flannel sheeting 18 inches wide, was the place of combat where I was to fight it out with my polio. I was still optimistic. I had been told mine was a light case, so I hoped that in two weeks I could be out of isolation. As yet, I still didn't realize what I was up against. But I also had an eerie feeling that I was about to be engulfed in a strange active abyss. Whatever it was, I could certainly feel its presence on the ward. My spine was cold and shivery. My muscles were tight and sore. My stomach was a knot.

The next two weeks were a nightmare to me. They grew from

two hot weeks into three weeks because my polio was turning out to be a strange kind called "progressive" and it had many tricks in store for me. It was a time marked mostly by the pain in my legs and in the small of my back. Nausea and vomiting were also an early part of this blur and delirium.

Usually, during the day the pain wasn't so bad because we were too busy to notice. Hot packs three times a day became an ungodly ordeal.

"What's that?" I asked the morning of the second day. A nurse had wheeled in a shiny cylinder about two and a half feet high and maybe eighteen inches in diameter. She began to plug in an electrical cord that came from the machine.

"Time for your hot packs," she replied.

"What are the hot packs for?"

"For you. To help you overcome your polio. Everybody gets them three times a day. It's part of the Sister Kenny treatment."

The cylinder began to whine. After a bit, some steam began to escape from under the lid. With the steam came an acrid, nauseating smell. I gagged.

"It's awful! What is it?"

"The flannel packs are trapping the steam. Soon the machine will shake the steam out of them. Watch."

No sooner had she said this than some kind of agitating process began to take place within the machine. The whine became piercing as the whole contraption shook. More vile smelling steam filled my end of the ward. My fascination for the behavior of the machine proved stronger than my nausea from the smell. I gagged twice more and waited.

"Take off your pajamas and just leave your shorts on," was the first command. The nurse greased me down with some kind of jelly-like substance. She anticipated my question.

"It's to keep you from burning."

"Burning?"

"These hot packs come out with live steam in them. The steam makes the flannel stink. The hot packs are 'hot' hot packs."

I was the first to receive this morning ablution, probably because it was my first time. The nurse took the top off the cylinder, and with a stick, like a yardstick, she fished out the hot pack. It was a green-brown piece of flannel, long since faded by the many, many steam applications. Its color was very compatible to my nausea. The flannel piece was body long and body wide, and it was still steaming and stinking as she laid it out on me from my neck down my back to my feet. I lay face down with my feet hanging straight down off the bottom of the bed.

The machine began to whine again as another pack began to stink. When my pack began to cool, and it took a long time for it to cool, the nurse rolled me over. This time, on my back, my feet had to be planted straight up on the footboard. At least she didn't cover my face with the pack but it came right up under my chin. I could feel one last gag not too far down.

I don't know how long the two packs lasted. Probably a half hour, but it seemed like an hour at least. By the time the packs were done, I was done. I was exhausted. I was drained.

The packs sapped my strength more than my polio did. They certainly took my mind off the pain. So it was that the whine of the packing machine began marking an unforgettable part of my day: a time after breakfast, a time after lunch and a time after dinner.

Every other day we had to fight it out with an enema. No one could go on his own, so enemas became part of our routine. After a while this whole event became doubly complicated as I encountered more and more difficulty trying to sit upon a bed pan. My legs were too tight and my back too stiff. I could hardly take the pain as I grew weaker. But I had my pride. I wanted to take care of my personal bodily functions all by myself for as long as I could. It was my will against the pain on the bed pan. But pride and the embarrassment of pride were a couple of things my polio cut down in a hurry.

My messages from the brain weren't getting through the disease in the spinal cord, so my lower body wasn't functioning. Still, I was lucky. As yet, I had not had to be catheterized. Some of the men around me weren't so fortunate. They were embarrassed, and they were uncomfortable. That was the first of many instances in which, by comparison, I considered myself well off. I didn't have to have a rubber tube sticking out of my penis, draining down to a jug under the bed. Not yet, anyway.

In addition to all this activity was the program of lying on my bed with my feet straight up against the footboard. The alternate strips of flannel and cotton sheeting across my bed were supposed to activate my nerves somehow and stimulate my sense of touch. I hated the flannel strips and tried to work my body around in the bed until my buttocks were on a cotton strip so I wouldn't sweat so much in all that heat.

The program called for keeping my feet absolutely flat on the footboard. It was not easy. It took will power to keep them flat. The pain became worse in my legs and I wanted to pull them up to ease the pain from my tightening hamstrings. It became more and more painful to keep my feet on the footboard.

My hamstrings were sticking out like bow strings in the back of my knee area when I kept my feet on the footboard. They were tightening. My hamstrings hurt more and more the tighter they became. It was easier to curl up my legs and forget the footboard so the pain would go away. Two men down a few beds from me had their feet strapped to their footboards so their legs wouldn't curl up and wither. They were in much pain as they writhed back and forth across their beds with their feet anchored to their footboards. Pain killers such as aspirin helped a little, but not much.

It was at night when the pain really did its work. I woke in the middle of the night and felt my legs twitching. The muscle spasms were running up and down them. It seemed as if the polio mice inside my leg muscles were holding mouse olympics. In the dark, I wondered what all this meant. I was fearful about what it was.

"Was my leg going out? Wiggle my toes. Nice little toes, still wiggling."

Funny thing, wiggling my toes. Probably wouldn't give it much thought in normal times, but suddenly, all the simple little things counted way up there. Can you imagine what it would be like to say to your big toe, "Move," and it wouldn't move? I wondered if I had lost it. Was my brain still in touch? And then I wondered if I had forgotten how to say to my toe, "Move," or to my insides, "Have a BM."

There was a deaf-mute patient on the ward with us. He was in for his third polio attack in three years. All his cases were light, without paralysis. The first day, before my polio really settled down to business with me, he came down to my bed and taught me the signing alphabet. We talked a bit this way. It was amusing for me and something to do but I worried about that man. Hadn't he already been afflicted with enough hardship without getting polio? But at least he could groan. He groaned along with the rest of us. We were all hurting.

The pain increased as the days went by; it narrowed down my awareness so that by the third day, I was condensed down to only me and my polio. The previous energy used brewing up visions of hardships gave way to getting on with the battle. Worry and fear were big parts of the fight, and sharing back and forth among us patients was one way of dealing with our fears. We tried to support each other as best we could, but none of us was exactly expert at it.

Down two stalls from me was Ed, a young farmer about my age. Both of his legs were out, and he wasn't doing very well from the waist down. During the war in the Pacific, he had received a gunshot wound in his left leg, and his polio was particularly attacking that weakness in his leg. His farm was up northwest of Omaha about 100 miles. My first night in the ward, Ed woke me up about midnight, calling his pigs in his sleep.

"Soowie? Soowie!" he called out quite clearly.

He repeated his calling out several times, until I called back, "Ed!" I called back four or five times before he woke up. I told him what he was doing.

"Yes, I was calling my pigs from the front porch back home," came his sleepy reply.

Ed came in a few days before me. When he had first become ill, the doctor had sent him home with the flu. A real bad case of the flu. But the medicine hadn't helped. He had been hoeing cockleburs in the milo and stacking prairie hay.

"It was mighty hot hoeing those cockleburs. And when you stack prairie hay, you really stack hay," he told me.

"I got so bent up, I took to walking around the farm with a big stick which I used as a combination cane and crutch. My head began to feel like it was being squeezed more and more in a big vice.

"Went to bed and about midnight, I woke up as it began to rain. I stumbled out into the pig yard where the brooding sows were. I shut up the piglets in the brood houses because wet piglets become sick piglets.

"I could just barely get my legs over the fence getting into the pig yard. I mean, I had to take a big breath and then strain hard to get a leg over the fence. It was quite a thing, reeling around out there what with all the lightning flashing, and the thunder rolling. One moment I could see where I was going, and the next I would stumble in darkness and hang onto the fence or my stick. The wind was blowing hard, too, and I just had a heck of a time out there. It was as though there was something awful big and black out there trying to get me down.

"Next morning, about seven, I sat up in bed. I don't remember feeling particularly bad, nothing worse, than what had been usual for the last few days. I got out of bed and fell down. I had a hard time getting up since Bernice wasn't there to help. She was in the hospital but was going to be released that day. I finally got up and fell down again. I fell down six times. I just couldn't figure out why I couldn't stay up.

"The neighbors found me crawling around outside in the barnyard. I was on my way to the outhouse, but I never made it. I was out of it. Outdoor biffies are always too far from the house. My brother-in-law came and took me to the hospital, and then he brought

Bernice home. I think I was pretty well gone by that time. Can't recall too clearly what went on.

"I got some kind of hot packs and some medicine there before I was brought down here by ambulance. The hot packs up there weren't anything like the ones we get here."

Ed's story came in fragments as he lay in bed fighting his polio. He didn't cry out much, but I could tell by his groans that the pain and worry were getting to him. He was particularly worried about his left leg where the gunshot wound was. But he kept talking as if he was going to go back to farming after he got out of the hospital.

CHAPTER THREE

Fear

On the other side of me was Osborne, a fine young man who was quite a high school football player from a small town about 75 miles southwest of Omaha. One of his legs was out and he was having some plumbing problems as well.

"I missed the fair. I missed the County Fair because of this dag blasted polio and I didn't get to show my prize lamb. I know I would have won the blue ribbon with her. I know football is out this year too, but it's missing the fair that really makes me disgusted!"

He volunteered this information right out on the first day as he reached up to hang onto the top of the glass partition between us. He had pulled himself up so he could look right at me. At that moment, I think his anger was stronger than any fear he might have had for his polio.

"I saw her born a year ago last March. It was in the morning when I was feeding hay to the sheep in the barn. We were having a sleet storm. I've seen lambs born before but there was something special about this one. I knew it right away, and told Dad I wanted to raise her in my 4-H program so I could enter her in the County Fair. She comes when I call and she stands real still when I brush her. But best of all, she is a real good looking lamb. I just know she would have won. The County Fair was yesterday."

He flopped back down on his bed more exhausted than he expected to be, judging from his big sigh.

It seemed as if none of us could get comfortable. Besides the pain in my muscles and hamstrings, my skin felt like it was on fire. Osborne and I couldn't stand the wool blankets and flannel strips.

Slowly, my legs were tightening. I knew it. I couldn't stop the hamstrings from pulling my feet off the footboard. I found myself becoming more and more helpless.

Osborne heard the ambulance coming before the rest of us did. The siren cut out as the ambulance turned into the hospital driveway. We could see out the window the tragedy below. There was a young woman in a respirator in the ambulance. Two medics were working her arms up and down. They rushed her into the hospital the moment the truck stopped. It wasn't long before we learned that she died as she entered the building. She had been married two weeks. That was the first of twenty-three polio deaths I was going to observe in that hospital in the next six weeks.

I had heard about the Fear of Polio stalking the land. Now I was seeing this fear. I was part of it! Now I had some understanding of why some mothers clutched their children to themselves and would not let them go to the crowded swimming pools or to the water-cooled movie theaters even when it was so beastly hot as it was then. How I wished we had some of that water cooling in our dismal, long gray ward instead of one rattling window fan, trying to keep the temperature in our ward down to the nineties at night.

Polio was raging in our midst, and mine had a vice grip on me. I found it was amazing what I had come to expect in that polio ward and what attitude I had come to accept in only a few days. This mystery was more than polio and hot weather linked together, although they certainly were suited to each other.

To me, hot weather now said, "polio" and polio now said, "hot weather, hot oppressive weather." It made me shiver to think that I had come to accept that attitude about my polio as though I was lying there and that was that. I was done. I was trapped.

Where had my mind gone? Where had my will to fight back against this thing gone? Polio was a terrible disease! It would lick me both in my mind and in my gut if I let it, and I couldn't tell if it was winning.

Osborne's abdominal muscles grew weaker. They had to catheterize him. I was having my plumbing troubles, too. I didn't want any tube stuck in me. Osborne said it was more uncomfortable than it was painful. But the nurses had to change the tube in him twice a day to keep it lubricated with surgical jelly so his inside skin wouldn't start sticking to it. Can you imagine being very pleased with the fact that you could still urinate all by yourself without help? And thankful too! Well, it wasn't so strange to feel that way in that ward where I was.

Along with the grief, there was another side to our polio experience. Right in the middle of our pain, we did have our lighter moments. These moments were often associated with urinals and bed pans. A student nurse would come bouncing in just as one of us was ready to do business with a urinal. Urinating then had become a major endeavor for all of us, and to be successful with a urinal was quite an achievement. I mean, not only did I have to strain my muscles, I had to concentrate with great effort on what I was doing. There even came a time for a bit of inner dialogue con job on myself.

"Come on, you can do it! You still have what it takes. Easy does it. You're on your way. Do it now. Push!"

At first, the appearance of a student nurse stopped my production. I became self-conscious, looked off into space and pretended that I really didn't want to use the darn thing after all. After a while, it didn't matter so much.

Modesty and embarrassment faded. Not only was I finding out that there were many different levels of paralysis to my polio, I was also finding that there was a switch to one part of my paralysis; modesty no longer kept me from going.

Sometimes conversation with Osborne followed a natural twist of humor. It came out the day I talked to George, on the other side of me. We both had visited Los Angeles in the last couple of years, and we admitted that our understanding had been greatly increased as to what real traffic was, and what it was like to drive in it. Big freeways were beginning to come in, and both of us had been impressed by what we had seen. Driving in Los Angeles was driving in a world different from the Midwest.

Osborne was listening to all of this, and perhaps he detected some kind of bragging on our part in the telling of our experiences in the Los Angeles traffic or perhaps he just didn't want to feel left out. Whatever, he did not remain silent.

"Heck, that's nothing. Why, down in Talmage we get some pretty big traffic jams on Saturday nights. It's been getting a lot worse in the last few years."

"Is that right?" replied George. "How many traffic lights do you have in town?"

"One," said Osborne.

"How far does traffic back up on a red light?"

"Once saw six cars, but it doesn't get that bad very often."

There was some silence.

"Well, we're supposed to be getting a second traffic light sometime next year. Yes, we are."

George and I tried to tell him what a freeway was. Slowly, he got the picture and was able to laugh a bit at himself, but he was still proud of that second traffic light going in.

Ed wasn't saying much. He seemed to be thinking about his two bum legs and his farm with all the crops and the pigs that were needing his attention. His wife, Bernice, could do some chores but she was still weak from her bout in the hospital.

Ed seemed to do more worrying than the rest of us because he had more responsibilities. But once in a while he and Osborne got going back and forth about planting crops or the ins and outs of tractors and cars. They both knew mechanics well and sometimes when George and I tried to get into the conversation with our limited understanding of mechanics, it was about as sad as Osborne trying to relate Talmage traffic to that in Los Angeles. So it came to be that there was a good deal of give and take among us at our end of the ward. We learned a little and shared some things.

After four or five days on the ward, we were fairly well settled down to a routine and most of us showed some signs of getting better or, certainly, not getting any worse. My back and legs weren't quite so tight, and Ed could move one of his legs just a bit. Not much, but a little, and as long as he could manage some movement in it, he was greatly encouraged. All of us seemed to be more hopeful.

There came a morning when Osborne let out a whoop and proudly announced to the world at large, and to us in particular, that he had just used the urinal all by himself. He was a proud young man. Every new shift of nurses that came on the floor received Osborne's glad tidings. Even the girls in the ward across the hall were tickled by this news announcement.

Before long, we were introduced to our physical therapist, the P.T. She soon earned the title "Bone Crusher" because it felt like she was bruising and battering us as she stretched hamstrings and muscles. She was a good person and a good therapist even though she was rough. We were all loosened up with some stretching and mild perseverance. In two days she had me up and walking as much as half the length of the ward. I was elated! I was going to get out of there in two weeks after all!

She was the one who explained to me what polio did and how it attacked. "The disease attacks the nervous system, not the muscles. Most of the cases are spinal polio. Polio attacks the spinal cord and blocks the messages from the brain to a finger or toe, for example. If the message can't get through, then the muscles making the toe or finger work will shrivel up. Your hamstrings tightening means your legs and feet and toes might shrivel up, either partly or completely.

"The other kind of polio is called 'bulbar' because it attacks the round pituitary gland at the base of the brain. Here, the polio blocks the messages to organs rather than to the muscles. It is the more dangerous of the two. You could be put into an iron lung because your lungs weren't getting the message, or you could be in the iron lung because the muscles making the lungs work received no message. It could even be a combination of both, and the doctors aren't always sure which is which.

"The fear polio brings out in people is startling sometimes. I know of a couple traveling west from Omaha not so long ago who were turned away from staying at a cabin camp because they were from Omaha. The people running the cabin camp told the couple they heard how terrible the polio was in Omaha and were afraid to let them stop for fear that they might catch the polio from the couple. You know how sparse towns are in the western part of the state. The couple had to travel far into the night before they finally found a place to rest. They kept quiet this time about being from Omaha."

It was good to have the PT close at hand, for there came a terrible change. On my sixth night, the pain shot back worse than ever before. With the pain this time came the fear from knowing what the awful symptoms meant. My back was killing me once again. There was no place in my bed where I could even begin to get comfortable. My legs were tight, and the footboard was an even harder target to achieve then before. My legs and thighs were burning up in a way different from before.

The muscle spasms were back, and I was afraid. Terribly afraid. The noises of the night began to play on my mind. I listened to a baby crying with diphtheria down the hall. She was really having a bad time with her tight cough. Ed was talking in his sleep about getting in the corn and shipping the pigs to market. Then, I realized there was something in my bed that was stronger than I was. My feet were beginning to come off the footboard.

It was the same nightmare all over again. Sleep seemed to be impossible.

"Wiggle little toes. Oh, how glad I am that I can still move you." I couldn't move them much, but I knew I could move them, and that was very important.

But now there came a new noise on the ward. At the far end was a patient who had just come out of the iron lung room. He was now in a respirator that was pulsing out its steady hiss as it helped him breathe. As I lay there in the dark, sweating in the heat of the hot night, I listened to the rhythm of the respirator. The hiss of the machine gradually became transformed into a heavy whispering voice over the rattle of the window fan. The husky whisper from the machine came with a cadence that drummed a horrible message into my blurring mind, "You're next. You're next." On that hot night, that is what it said to me, and I almost believed it. I feared I was going to be the next in that infernal machine! I wanted to get away from there! Sleep seemed to escape me, and yet I did wander off into a semi-consciousness where I was aware of just one thing, the pain! Coupled with the pain this time was the fear. Back and forth across the bed I went, trying to find a comfortable place. Wouldn't the pain ever stop?

Weary, in the morning, I tried to raise a glass of water for a drink. My arm and hand went out of control. I could barely hold the glass, but my arm and hand shook so much, all the water spilled out. I had another spinal tap that day. I didn't know what was going on.

I was vaguely aware that I could not curl up enough to get the vertebrae spread enough so the needle could easily reach the spinal cord. This time, the whole experience hurt. Then came a deep nauseating feeling. A numbing headache followed, and I was all but out of it. My humanity became a blur.

What did the cell count show? I wanted to know what was happening. I was getting worse while the rest were getting better! Sometime during the day the PT told me that I had what was called "progressive" spinal polio; this was probably the real attack.

The spinal fluid showed that I still had active polio. All the recovering I had gone through had been for nothing. I had to start all over again. Maybe I would have even more attacks later on and perhaps not. There was no telling with my kind of polio. Mine was not like most polio cases when a person knew within 24 to 48 hours what damage the savage attack of polio had done. Thereafter, all the effort was directed towards recovery. But my polio wouldn't leave me alone and be done with me. I was weak, very weak. I was afraid. It was awful being afraid. I struggled on in a rarefied atmosphere.

Fear had blown away almost all notion of peace or comfort on my ward. Whatever comfort prevailed, came mostly from my doctor, Rich Young. He was an old family friend. But Rich was dying of Parkinson's disease, the disease that inflicts the terrible shakes on a person and then makes that worse with tightening muscle rigidity. Rich had been a handsome man before the disease struck, but now he was gaunt. A high squeaky voice had replaced a full-bodied baritone. But even so afflicted himself, he was the doctor who came to see me every morning on the ominous isolation ward.

He didn't need to do that. He was exposing himself to the ravages of polio each day he came. He already had enough grief in his life. He was terminal. He was wealthy and could have traveled extensively. He might have spent more time with his family or on a hobby. But he was coming in to see me and other patients each day. And as his muscles didn't work so well either because of his disease, it was easy to tell when he came upon the floor.

I could hear him shuffling down the long ward. He was leaning forward as though he was struggling to get ahead into the face of a strong wind in a storm. His steps were jerky. Under the circumstances, it appeared as though the addition of his affliction to the tragedy already going on about our ward would hardly have lent itself to any kind of comfort or reassurance.

He carried one of those little chrome hammers with the red, hard rubber triangle-shaped head. He used it to test my reflexes at my knee and ankle. Each time he drew back to tap me, the hammer would shake badly in his hand. It seemed impossible that he could ever strike the blow to its mark. Yet each time the hammer struck true. His spirit was in control of his body, even if his flesh was weak. There was something hidden under the visibly shaking frame that was very strong. In spite of his outward and visible distraction from the disease, something within him that seemed to master not only his own shaking frame but also the hubbub and anxiety on our ward.

Even when he couldn't get any reaction out of my knees or ankles from the strike of the hammer, he would still look me right in the eye and in his sing-song voice, he would ask, "Bob, are you all right?"

And no matter how bad it hurt, even on my worst day, the day my left arm went out and I spilled the water, I felt as if I had to say, "Yes."

He said this to me every morning; and no matter how badly I felt, no matter how rough the night before had just been, no matter how much it hurt or how much anxiety I was feeling over spending the rest of my life in a wheelchair, his question, "Bob, are you all right?" always made me answer, "Yes."

And the "yes" I was answering wasn't just a passing-the-time-of-day kind of "yes." It was a real answer. It was my answer being given in response to something that caused me to consider more than simply my poor body. I wasn't being philosophical, I was making a total response, and it was as simple as that.

This man had something. I don't know whether or not he was manipulating me to say "yes" for my own good, but at the time, I didn't feel that way at all. What I felt was the kindness of this man. He was capable of conveying to me his total compassion. He was giving me his strength, and that is a funny thing to say about a man who was in the shape he was in. I felt that if anyone could really know how I felt, he did.

When he inquired, "Bob, are you all right?" I received the most sincere searching kindness possible, and this came from him over and over again. It was part of his nature, and while he repeated it every day, it never became commonplace. Maybe his long suffering had deepened his ability to be compassionate and kind. This kindness of his was not in any way dramatic. Rather, it was reassuring, a kind of building experience that made me feel stronger. Each day my strength increased when he came shuffling in to see me.

This is what I know: He could have come down with polio himself. Enough professional people around us did. He was bad enough off as it was without asking for more trouble. He could very well have sent one of his associates or one of the interns to see me and check my reflexes. But he didn't. He came himself, and I think he was coming to check out something more than my reflexes.

CHAPTER FOUR

Dennis and Johnny

Once again, I wondered how tight my legs could become. My hamstrings were bowed so tight they were tearing. I had reached my limit and I could not keep my feet on the footboard. This bothered me terribly because I knew I should keep my feet on that footboard so my legs wouldn't shrivel up. My right calf was shriveling.

It was my will against the polio, and I was losing. It eased the pain so much to curl my legs, but, even doing that, I couldn't get comfortable. I really didn't want to spend the rest of my life in a wheelchair, but I just couldn't keep my feet on that board. I suffered from a great deal of anxiety. I hurt in my body and deep inside as well. "Is it in my pride or in my soul where the fear is?"

By the end of the day, my left arm was just a little bit better. Actually, the weakness in the arm was a much more dangerous symptom than any other I had had because the nerve to the arm was closely associated with the one going to the lung. My left arm had been badly damaged in a recent automobile accident, and perhaps that was why my polio chose to attack that arm rather than the right one.

Whatever the reason, the misery was upon me, and I was in much pain. The hot packs continued. The despair of weakness grew, and the stretching with the PT began again. This time it hurt terribly in the hamstrings when she pulled my feet down straight but I had lost all feeling and movement in my feet. I couldn't wiggle my toes! No little toes to wiggle. My hamstrings were on fire when she stretched me. This time, I came very close to having the catheter. I became delirious during that second week.

Even though this last blast had come upon toward the beginning of the second week, I was still to be released to the convalescing ward at the end of the third week. Recovery for me during the third week was minimal. I stabilized. The staff felt they had done all they could for me with the hot packs and the stretching. The hot packs left me very weak.

Before I was released from isolation, I had to be disinfected. So did *Across the Wide Missouri*, the book that I had brought in with me. It shriveled. Taking the disinfecting bath became a very painful task. It was hard for me to sit up so I could get into a wheelchair for the ride to the tub. It was harder yet for me to climb up from the wheelchair into the tub. My muscles were screaming. Even with help, it felt like I was tearing them as I made those difficult moves. An aide named Rick helped me. Once in the tub though, the sensation of floating in the water was absolutely wonderful. Lying there in the water, the pressure was off my skin and my muscles. I didn't want to leave. My body told me it wanted to stay and soak it all up.

Both Ed and Osborne had moved into the convalescent ward a few days before me, so it was good being with them again on that much smaller ward. There was something symbolic about moving into that new ward. It faced east so we could see the sun rise. We saw some beautiful sunrises from there. It was also cooler in the afternoon shade. All of this was helpful because even the slightest comfort was greatly appreciated. My body still hurt that much.

The first night, I found it necessary for me to become accustomed to two new noises. One was the noise of the respirator on Dennis, and the other was his coughing. Dennis was the patient who had been at the far end of our isolation ward in that respirator. It was his hissing respirator that whispered to me, "You're next," Now he was only a few beds down from me, so I had to cope with both the hiss and his cough at close quarters.

Dennis was all right during the day, for he could manage comfortably outside the respirator, but it was at night that his noises filled the ward. The dark seemed to amplify them. I dreaded hearing the respirator again that night. I knew I was up tight about it. His weak wet cough was something new for me. It made me want to clear my own throat.

Dennis had been in the iron lung and now had graduated to the respirator. That's why he hadn't been in our isolation ward very long before he came into this convalescent ward. Now he used the respirator only while sleeping. About a week earlier, he had caught a cold, which naturally had gone into his chest. That threw back his recovery about two weeks.

Since Dennis could not cough effectively by himself, Rick, the ward boy, helped him cough by placing both of his hands flat on Dennis' chest. Then he pushed down with a short sharp push. Not much happened with the first push, but a mild cough could be heard. It slurped. Rick repeated the motion as he and Dennis seemed to set up a rhythm until a kind of coughing began. This gave the appearance of artificial respiration from the front. After a while the coughing began to sound as if it might be producing something down inside. Ever so slowly, I could hear the phlegm making its progress up his throat with each push by Rick. Every one of us in the ward worked that phlegm up as we listened to its progress. I'm sure most of us on the ward cleared our own throats several times during the passage of Dennis' phlegm.

That phlegm coming up in Dennis' throat made a lovely sound, particularly when it finally reached the back of his throat and began to gurgle and sputter. From that point on, there was usually a final slurp followed by a few fast gagging noises, and then Dennis had it in his mouth. Rick wiped it out.

Then the two of them would have a conversation about whether or not it was a "good one." Sometimes, I suspected, they kept score. After two or three of these sessions, Rick would strap on the respirator and put Dennis to bed.

I thought my first night on this new ward was going to be a tough one, but the steady breathing of the machine soon lulled me to sleep. Nor was there a weak cough. And no dreadful whispering voice this time telling me, "You're next." This was such a delightful change from my earlier experience in the isolation ward. My weary body needed this encouragement.

Dennis was a favorite of many people in the hospital. Often, there were two or three people at his bedside down there at the other end of the ward. Perhaps that was so because he needed so much attention. Neither one of his arms worked very well. His left arm had some strength, but his right arm was out except for some slight movement in three of his fingers.

He was one of the most emaciated persons I had ever seen. He had traveled a terrible path to be that way. He had lost 55 pounds since going into the iron lung just over a month before.

He was the only one in the hospital who came out of the iron lung alive that summer. Maybe that was why he received so much attention, but I thought it was also because he was such a fine person. Dennis and I developed a friendship on that ward, and I felt good about being around him.

It was a whole new routine in the convalescent ward than on the isolation ward, and it was so much more enjoyable. Warm baths replaced the hot packs. The night nurses didn't have to wear masks anymore, and our night nurse turned out to be a beauty. But the big change for us was that we could have visitors twice a week. My aunt and uncle came and brought me some ice cream. They told me about Nancy's wedding. The reception had been delayed until they returned from their honeymoon because it was to be held at the house where I had had the polio attack. We just didn't know how polio was carried then, or if it even was carried. So Nancy and Bob came home to enjoy their reception all rested from their honeymoon. They sent me a fancy card from some gold mining place in Colorado.

Some of my friends came too, and they tried to make light of my whole illness. They tried to keep their visit on the light side to help cheer me up as good friends will do.

"You have the greatest propensity for adversity of anyone I know," was one of the comments.

That was one of the one-liners I could remember, but my friends were truly disturbed by my condition. I couldn't sit up straight then, and I couldn't walk. I had no feeling in my feet. I couldn't move my toes either. My friends went away uneasy. It was too spooky to have many visitors with polio rumbling around. No one really knew what kind of risks were being taken by making a visit.

Those first visits greatly emphasized the fact that we had been in another world. We had been in a raging hell. Our being in that other world of isolation was an unspoken reality on both sides.

There were questions on both sides of those first encounters: "Will he be the same?" "Will he look different?" "Will my shriveled leg make any difference?" "Am I still a whole person?" It was usually the look in the eyes of visitors that set off our anxiety feelings the most. There was that long searching look meant to penetrate our innermost thoughts. The loved ones who came wanted to share what had happened to us. Obviously something extremely significant had taken place, but they hadn't been involved in it. Sometimes they even exhibited a more upsetting cat-like watching.

How often we wished they would just pounce and ask us if we were afraid or if it hurt. But they didn't. They were only anxious to help, to share our feelings which we usually found difficult to express. But, because they didn't know what we had been through, they could only imagine what it was like. Their imagined specters created worry and tension, which showed in their anxious faces. It was their silent looks that so often raised barriers between us.

Rich Young was so fascinated by these almost ritualized meetings that he made a study of the behavior of parents and closely associated relatives and friends of polio patients, which he published in *Mental Hygiene*. He discovered that, far more than other illnesses, families suffered anxiety over polio and the fear of the unknown. That was probably because, while the polio patients were zeroed in on only one thing—fighting polio—the families felt helpless. We were in a storm, they weren't. We doing something in the fight; they couldn't.

But my mother tried. She came back from California and took a job at the hospital as a nurse's aid. She was then able to slip into our ward several times a day when she could grab some spare time. The work was heavy for her, but she managed. She knocked herself out on the job for 12 to 14 hours a day so she could be near me and provide some extra comfort. Sometimes her doing for me was almost too much.

I had this feeling that she was always just off stage in the wings, hovering. She seemed ready to fly to my aid at any moment should I indicate by any gesture that I was unable to do something for myself. I had to do the recovering, but it was good seeing her. We hadn't seen each other for four years except for the graduation in June.

The hot baths were fine. No, they were great! I could relax in the big tub and move my arms back and forth with ease. My legs had some feeling, but there was not much movement. I worked at trying to move my legs in the water. I managed a little action back and forth.

The tub was called a "butterfly tub" because it was shaped for big arm and leg action. Lots of room. It was great to move my legs again. I think Ed liked the tub more than any of the rest of us. That seemed so because it was so darn difficult getting him out of there so the rest of us could have our turns. His bad leg moved a little in the tub. That was encouraging because he couldn't get any movement out of it on the bed. He said he was trying to make an arrangement so he could sleep in the tub!

The pressure of the water made it difficult for Dennis to breathe in the tub, but, even so, he looked forward to his daily hot bath. All of us did. Going to the bath gave us a chance to get out of the ward, go down the hall and see other patients. As we went by, we often struck up conversations.

It was interesting in our hospital, how each person's case was supposed to be private, known only by the doctor and the nurses, yet many of us knew how a patient was doing. Call it the grapevine. Though I hadn't been officially notified that Linda wasn't keeping her feet on the footboard, every time I went by her room in my wheelchair, I asked her if she was being a good girl.

"It's hard for me to keep my feet on this mean old board," she said. "My legs hurt too much. But I'm keeping them on it some. That's better than it was."

For a ten-year-old, she was doing fine, and she was getting better. She was cute, and she knew it. Her four-year-old brother Johnny was also cute but not in a cute way. He became an entirely new dimension on our ward. He had been moved into our ward as part of the overflow from Children's Hospital. Smart for his age—and he was quick—he was also only four years old. He took one look at all of us on the ward and decided he didn't fit in. We tried to ease him into our daily routine, but he had his own ideas. He was stubborn about what he was and was not going to do. It wasn't so much his getting used to us as it was our getting used to him. Because he was placed next to me with the wall on his other side, I became his only conversationalist.

He started right out with his inquiries, and it didn't look as if he'd ever let up. He wanted to go home. I hoped he would soon. I tried to teach him a few things, and he educated me. For 24 hours a day he went on; some days it seemed longer than 24 hours. I really did expect him to run down and become quiet, but he never did. "Because" was his answer to questions, and "Why?" was his question to my answers. I no sooner answered one of his questions then he came at me again with "Why?" I wondered why the word was ever invented.

Johnny played his top trick on us right at dinner time. He received his dinner first on our ward, and, about half way through, he had to have either a urinal or a bed pan, usually the latter. He had to have a bedpan just as we were receiving our dinner, or just as Rick or Metch was about to feed Dennis. So they stopped to answer Johnny's need and Dennis' food got cold. Dennis tried to lay down the law to Johnny about his bedpan routine at dinner time with little success.

"Johnny, can you wait until dinner is over before you have your bedpan?"

Dennis' voice wasn't all that strong. If Johnny did hear, he didn't act as though he did. He simply withdrew into the world of a child. He faced the wall and wouldn't be reached. Maybe he needed some kind of attention.

Dennis even tried talking to him at another time about this bedpan routine but to no avail. There was not much room to reason with him. It was either the urinal or bedpan or else! Johnny had much power with this leverage, and he used it.

Johnny was in good shape when he came on our ward. His legs were a little stiff, and he did have some weakness in his plumbing, but, fortunately, there was no bad paralysis. Just one bad condition that came on at dinner time. My own opinion was that he could have gone home the day he came in with us. And the one thing he made perfectly clear from the beginning was that he wanted to go home. He kept telling us that.

His only bad time of day was when he first woke up. Then he was fussy and ornery for about fifteen minutes until he was fully awake. After that he was all right.

I quickly got him squared away with the notion that the only way he was going to go home was by being good and doing what the doctors and nurses told him to do. It started this way:

"Keep your feet on the footboard."

"Why?"

"Johnny, feet kept on the footboard mean no stretching is needed by the PT. That means getting well sooner, which means going home sooner."

"I didn't know that."

He started keeping his feet on the footboard. It was almost too easy. Then we went to work on his crying for a bedpan or a urinal. He didn't have a light to signal the nurse; none of us had signal lights. So he had to call for the things he needed. Crying had become his habit. He had a whiny cry, and it irritated me. I pointed out to him that a whine from his end of the ward probably wasn't going to be heard too well.

"I need a urinal," came his first attempt, little more than a whimper.

"Louder," I said. "They'll never hear you. What are you crying for?"

"I need a urinal." It was becoming a little more positive.

"That's better. Speak out like a man. Yell like hell!"

"What's hell?"

"You can tell your mother that you've been there and back again simply by being in this place with your polio."

I had heard the adage: "A picture is worth a thousand words." Something like that happened to Johnny, and I was the picture. After almost a month in that hospital with my polio, my GI tract finally got retracked. I climbed upon a bedpan one morning as was usual. I filled it and called out loudly for another. Johnny was watching. I filled that one and called out loudly for another pan. I was almost apologetic, but I was also feeling better and better. I kept calling until six bedpans had been carried away. I couldn't believe it and neither could Johnny. He had his lesson in how to call out for a bedpan.

Sometimes he asked questions just to get attention. But he caught on quickly, and, quite soon, he could yell fairly well for the necessities of life. Sometimes he lapsed back into his whine, but not too often. It was a quick little cry as though he was trying to keep it to himself as much as possible. I often let him cry it out, and usually after a short time he was quiet. This quiet lasted for a spell. Then, "Bob, when am I going home?"

"I don't know."

"When am I going to see my mother?"

"Sunday."

"Bob, how many days until Sunday?"

It didn't take him long to learn every day of the week, when it came and how long it was going to be until he saw his mother. Sunday was going to be the first time he had seen his mother and father in two weeks. We tried to cheer him up until then. I told him some stories from *Winnie the Pooh* and *The Jungle Book* that I could remember. Johnny liked Mother Wolf. I read his mail to him, and he received quite a bit. I think most of us went a little out of our way for him because he was without family and playmates. I certainly was not a four-year-old's playmate. Being next to Johnny could be tiring, and sometimes it certainly was!

CHAPTER FIVE

Learning, and a Diploma

Our routine at night included listening to the full round of murder and detective stories on the radio. When Johnny first encountered this, he protested loudly, which he reinforced with some crying.

"Oh, no!" I thought to myself. "Not this, too!"

We all went to work on Johnny to give in, and the thing that tipped the scale with him came when we pointed out that the good guys always won. The really hard part came when we tried to get him used to the squeaky doors of "Inner Sanctum."

"That scares me! It sounds like ghosts."

We tried naked strategy, "It doesn't scare me," and "It's fun to be scared a little. It's just a radio, Johnny."

We didn't win that one. That is, we didn't talk him into agreeing to listen. He listened, but he didn't like it at first. Monday nights became firmly etched in his mind. He knew when Mondays came as well as when Sundays came. I think that by the time he went home he could take the squeaky doors of "Inner Sanctum" in his stride, and as for the usual run-of-the-mill murders on the detective programs, he hardly noticed.

A week on this ward did wonders. We were all doing better. I could almost sit up straight. Ed and Osborne were moving around well in wheelchairs. Ed was having some difficulty getting his farm chores done at home, and it looked to me as if it was going to be a long time before he got back to that kind of work. Osborne wasn't going to be playing football soon, if ever, but even so, we could all see some progress. It was certainly a bright ward.

27

Even Dennis' rattling cough was getting better, and the PT began to argue with Dennis about taking away the respirator at night. He really didn't need it any longer, and he did realize that, at least in his head.

"I'm afraid to go without it. I have this fear that I'll choke in my sleep without its breathing for me. I'm dependent on it and can't break away."

So what did the PT do? She waited for Dennis to take his afternoon nap in the respirator, and after he fell asleep, she turned it down as low as it would go. There were no mishaps. He did just fine in his sleep that way. Was he ever pleasantly surprised! So that night, he was going to try sleeping without it. I could see real concern in his face, but I think he knew there would be people close by most of the night. Even Johnny understood what was happening. He had decided Dennis wasn't such a bad guy after all.

In the morning Johnny asked, "Bob, did Dennis make it through the night ok?

"I think he did, Johnny. I didn't hear him cough once." Dennis was tired that morning. His night had been restless, but he had made it through safely. He was wearing a happy but tired face. He had finally graduated from the respirator. That night, he put this poem above his bed, or to be more accurate, he had Metch put it up there for him.

Now I lay me down to sleep,
I lay the respirator at my feet.
If I should gasp before I wake,
Strap it on for heaven's sake!

That was his self-designated diploma. How could he ever receive a better one? Everyone felt good about what had happened to Dennis. It had been a big day also because Ed left us to go down to the V.A. hospital in Lincoln. With Osborne leaving on crutches the day before, I now found myself more confined to Johnny. I had suggested to the nurses that Johnny and I be moved up next to Dennis and I thought they would do that the next day. That was also the day I was to have my fourth spinal tap and I was really uptight about that, and with good reason.

My third spinal tap came the day I moved on to that ward. It was done by a technician who may or may not have been an intern. Whether he was or wasn't was almost beside the point. His bungling of that third spinal tap erased almost all my confidence in his ability to do the job correctly.

On the third day of my tap, he pushed his medical cart down

our ward with his test tubes and other things of glass jiggling and rattling. Up to that moment in the hospital, I had no reason to fear or be uncomfortable about a spinal tap. I cooperated by curling up as best I could after he gave me a couple of shots of novocain in my lower back. The shots smarted as usual. So far, everything was progressing as usual as I lay there curled up, waiting for the tap. But then I became aware of the man's hands fumbling around on my lower back. His fumbling seemed to go on for a long time. It was much longer than during the previous taps. He finally mumbled something like, "I hope this goes right" and the next thing I could feel was a dull sensation as he applied the needle to the spinal cord. All at once, my body shuddered, and my right arm involuntarily jerked up into the air. I experienced a deep nauseating sensation in my stomach as the technician said, "Oh, I guess I missed. I'll try again. Hold real still."

I thought to myself, "What does he think I'm doing?"

I know I tightened up after this shock, and it took him a long time to draw the fluid out without any more antics on his part. It was after this tap that I experienced my first residual headache. It lasted the rest of the day, and the nausea stayed with me until dinner time. It scared me because the sensations were very much like coming down with polio all over again.

With this experience still fresh in my mind, I was not exactly looking forward to my next experience with "the butcher," as I had come to call this technician. I was sure he had some idea of how I felt about him, and this knowledge probably made him all the more tense about doing this fourth tap.

I was going to have the tap before Johnny and I moved up next to Dennis. I tried really hard not to look at the technician or to convey any of my uneasiness. Johnny watched fascinated.

"Does it hurt, Bob?"

"No, it's not bad, Johnny," I said, trying to reassure myself as well as him. The spinal tap took a long time, longer than last time, but this time no mishaps. The man went away with his cart jiggling again, and I hoped he would come up with better news than the last time I had that spinal tap. That time, the fluid showed signs that my polio was still active within me but not in great force. I didn't understand why the polio was still active in me.

Shortly before we moved up to be with Dennis, Johnny had an accident which I felt sure he could have avoided. He soiled his bed rather than calling out for a bedpan.

"You're a bad boy, and you should be spanked."

He winced and turned his head to the wall.

"You'd better call Metch so she can clean it up before there is a bigger mess."

"Metch," he called in his old weak little voice, not the usual strong voice he had come into lately. Then after a bit, with a quivering lip, he asked, "Bob, why am I a bad boy?"

He sounded hurt, but I also heard a real desire to know why.

"Why?" I was absolutely flabbergasted. Why anyone knew better than that. Well . . . It was . . .

"My aching back," I thought to myself, "this is going to be a good one, and he wants an answer.

"Well, Johnny, it's like this. You are a bad boy because you have made a mess that one of the nurses has to come in and clean up. This takes time, valuable time when she might be doing something else. I know you can call out for a bedpan. Maybe while she is cleaning up your mess, she could be helping someone who is very sick, maybe even help someone who is dying.

"But now, because you have had this accident, which we both know probably could have been avoided, you have taken up time with one of the nurses that might have been better spent.

"Now Johnny, you know that sometimes you have to wait a long time before a nurse comes here to help you when you really need help. This is because there just aren't that many nurses in this hospital. There aren't enough to do the job to get us all well at the same time. And these nurses have to be where they can do the most good. Cleaning up your mess isn't doing the most good.

"There is a little boy about your age down the hall with bulbar polio. This is the worst kind of polio there is. It is an awful thing, Johnny, what he has. He is lying head down on a bed tilted high in the air."

"Why is his bed tilted high in the air, Bob?"

"He has a very hard time breathing and because this is so, the nurses have to put a tube up his nose giving him oxygen down in his lungs, down here, right here, so he can breathe."

Johnny looked at me as I showed him where his lungs were.

"He has tubes stuck in each arm to feed him because his throat muscles have collapsed and he can hardly swallow. The tubes bring liquid to him so he won't dry up in this heat. We don't want him to get dehydrated. His bed is tilted high in the air so the phlegm will run down his throat so he can spit it out. Remember how Rick helps Dennis to cough by pushing down on his chest?"

"Yes, Bob, I know. That's to get the bad stuff out of him so he won't die."

"That's right, Johnny. Well, the bed tilted up helps the phlegm come out of the boy in much the same way. With the bed tilted up, the phlegm runs out of his lungs, up his throat and into his mouth so he can spit it out. And then there are some more tubes stuck in his legs to draw some fluid out because he doesn't go to the bath-room so good. So they help him this way too.

"Johnny, he is a very sick boy and he may die. He doesn't cry very much. Maybe he can't cry any more because his throat muscles are weak. But you know what, Johnny, he had a smile on his face when I went by in my wheelchair on my way to take my bath early this morning. Very few people live to tell of such an experience as he is going through right now. He needs to have nurses helping him all the time. You can help him have nurses by being a good boy and doing the right thing."

"Bob, do you mean that I can help that boy by not being a bad boy like this?"

"That's right Johnny, you can."

"Then I promise I'll be a good boy. And you know what? I won't even cry any more."

That was a promise Johnny kept except for a couple of times when he was grouchy in the morning and was constipated with a good deal of pain. Other than that, he kept to his word. I was proud of him.

After moving up next to Dennis, I found that Johnny was a great source of amusement to us. We couldn't resist egging him on to ask for an electric urinal and such whenever Metch or Rick came onto the floor. But the most pleasure he gave us came by his quickness in learning things.

"Reason," was a word he had fun with. It replaced "because" in his conversation. Sometimes Dennis' questions were too heavy, and about the only way Johnny could respond was with "because." Dennis told Johnny, " 'because' is not a reason. You have to have a reason for doing something, Johnny. What reason will you have for going home?"

"Because."

"That is not a reason. The reason you're in the hospital is be-cause you have polio. Now, you're recovering. What will the reason be for your going home? Why will you be going home? What is the reason?"

"Because I'll be all better. Because I'll be well."

The flash of his smile and the twinkle of his blue eyes told us he knew he understood his reason for going home.

"Now you know what a reason is. The reason you will go home is that you are well."

Dennis and I then set out to see if Johnny had learned his lesson well in reasoning. The word "difference" was our word. Johnny said he knew what the word meant.

"What is the difference between a man and a woman?"

"A man has black hair and a woman has light hair."

"What's the difference between a woman and a girl?"

"Girls have long hair and women wear glasses."

"You'll have to do better than that. You have to have a better reason for the difference between a woman and a girl."

"Women wear high heels and girls don't."

"Anything else?"

"Women wear silk stockings and girls don't."

"Good, Johnny. Now you know some reasons for the difference."

He didn't stop with working on our ideas, he came up with some of his own. After listening to the song "I'm Laughing on the Outside but I'm Crying on the Inside," Johnny said to the two of us, "Hey, you know what? That's me. I'm laughing on the outside but I'm crying on the inside."

He looked back and forth at each one of us to see if he had it right. He could tell right away that he did by the way we were looking at him.

The time came for Johnny to move out of our ward and into the room with his sister Linda. That was a bit unusual having a brother and sister in the same room together, but it looked as if they both would be going home soon. That gave me more reason for stopping by the room where Linda was, now that Johnny was there too. She was doing much better, and, by then, I had developed a very professional attitude with Linda, checking her out to see how she was doing, like keeping her feet on the footboard.

One day I noticed she was sitting up in bed with her legs tucked up under her. That was a bad habit, for that posture encouraged tightening of the hamstrings. That day, however, she did not scurry to get her feet back on the footboard when she saw me coming. In a very loud authoritative voice, I greeted her.

"Well, Linda, I see you don't care about keeping your feet on the footboard. Sitting up cross-legged like that is very bad for your hamstrings, as we both know."

In an equally loud voice, quite surprising to me, she answered, "I can't get my feet on the footboard. I'm sitting on the bed pan." Her laugh was almost devilish.

Snickers came from rooms near-by where there were other women patients. Johnny laughed too.

"From now on," I said to Linda, "I intend to wear my glasses as I go to take my bath so I won't make the same kind of foolish mistake again. People here today in this hospital are enjoying a good laugh on me."

CHAPTER SIX

Life and Death

With Johnny's departure, only Dennis and I remained at our end of the ward. The isolation ward was packed, however. But for the moment, we had a quiet ward. I was sitting up in my wheelchair now, so I was able to read comfortably again. That gave me great pleasure. The book I was reading was *Across the Wide Missouri*, a great book about the Mountain Men in the West in the 1830s. We could almost see the Missouri River from our window. Whenever I came to a particularly interesting part, I took it upon myself to read aloud to Dennis, who seemed to enjoy it.

Because of this reading aloud, some of the nurses, nurses' aides, and ward boys dubbed me, "Buffalo Bob." I earned this distinction mainly from the time I spent reading to Dennis about the domestic life of the mountain men with their Indian wives. Upon looking up one time, I found about two-thirds of the nurses on the floor standing in the doorway. Their amusement at my reading to Dennis grew.

The nurses on our floor were a good group, a fine group. The only thing wrong with them was there were not enough of them. Our hospital was extremely short of help in general and of graduate nurses in particular. With a few ward boys and fewer nurses' aides, the whole group provided great service. Rick had assumed the role of taking care of Dennis during the day.

Rick was a good young man but quite a character as well. He had been taken off night duty because of his feared relationships with some of the women patients. There had been no complaints; his reassignment was a precautionary one. There was no doubt about it, he was a "wow" with the women. Both Dennis and I were picking up a few pointers from Rick. We were both hopeful of learning some of his moves.

It was amazing to see how much difference there was in getting things done when certain people were in charge of the floor. A few nurses could get things done well and quickly. Hillard, Norall and Holtz were three of the younger nurses who fell into that category of efficiency. They got results. We needed many more like them.

There came the day when I saw only Hillard and one ward boy on duty for an entire day shift on the whole floor on our side of the hospital. By herself she packed our entire floor in an hour and a half with only two packing machines. And I also saw Dennis call for a nurse for 10 minutes before Hillard could answer. There weren't enough people to go around to keep up with our needs. Sometimes the two of us broke out into the first few bars of "Where Are You Now That I Need You?" but the staff did not always enjoy our form of humor.

As I grew better and could navigate around in my wheelchair, I was able to help Dennis when he needed to have an arm shifted or turned over. But usually Metch and Rick took care of him. Metch was something special with Dennis. Even though she had gone through so much with Dennis since the iron lung room days, she still got after him if she found him feeling low or sorry for himself. His downers didn't come too often and usually Metch had a gleam in her eye as she saw Dennis displaying signs of improvement. He was something special to her.

It's often said that nurses and doctors become hardened to all the misery, death and pain about them day in and day out. After being around them for almost six weeks, I saw something else. They didn't usually talk openly about someone who dies or "expires" as the doctors preferred to put it, but I could sense their reactions and feelings.

I know they felt loss as much as anyone else, but they had to get on with their jobs and save the people they could. They showed their feelings in a different way. It was a hellish grind for those who were conscientious, and most of them were. I knew I had been around a group of truly fine people with but few exceptions.

Most of my pain was gone now and I was in the process of gaining back my strength. I was still very weak so I was trying to build up my leg muscles as well as continuing to stretch my hamstrings more and more. Light exercise, hot baths and the stretching were my routine along with afternoon baseball games and nighttime detective stories on the radio. Simply being able to sit up straight again without pain was a delightful luxury. I knew there was more hope in my outlook.

I spent more and more time up in the wheel chair reading and talking to Dennis and helping him smoke a cigarette in his holder. Sometimes I turned over one of his hands when it became uncomfortable. About all he could do for himself was hold the cigarette holder in his left hand. He couldn't lift his left arm up to his lips to puff on the cigarette in the holder. Once I got the arm up so he could puff, he couldn't put it back down again on the bed. It simply flopped if I let go. He could walk a little if there was someone to hold up his arms; otherwise, the weight of his dead arms was painful to the muscles in his chest.

As we became better acquainted, I learned more about what he had been through. The more I listened to him, the more I realized how fortunate I was. The wonderful aspect of Dennis was his spirit. It was almost impossible to get him down. He knew he was going to get well. For him, there was no alternative. He wouldn't have it any other way. I had to believe him when he told me he was going to get well. He had already come back from the iron lung, oxygen tube up his nose, suction pump down his throat, arms out, and the catheter.

He was entering the longer and slower stage of recovery when progress wasn't so noticeable. He had gained some weight back. He needed much more. Bones still stuck out on him. I could believe him when he told me he had lost 60 pounds. The single most encouraging thing about him was that he had most of his muscles intact. There were some very weak ones, but they were there and in time could be built back up, generally speaking.

Dennis was a good example of the one thing about polio which never varies. Patience was absolutely necessary. The disease didn't teach it to us; it required patience from us. I was not normally a patient person, so I was learning slowly. Recovery couldn't be hurried along. It had to be steady. There was a time for all things, as Dennis was showing me. He had relentless patience.

As I scratched my face one afternoon, hardly aware of what I was doing, I looked up to see Dennis watching me. "I'd give my right arm if I could do that."

"There's no bargain in that. Your right arm is worthless."

"Ah shutupa your face" came his reply. That was one of the lines from *Life with Luigi*, one of our favorite evening radio programs.

"Save me, save me, whata you think I am, the Salvation Army? Your armsa no good. Whata you wanta do, my fran, give me a bum trade?"

We often went on this way for quite a while, as we liked the program and its Italian jargon so much. We almost always ended up the same way. We had to have proof of Dennis' physical prowess by demonstration. We put out his right arm to see what his right hand could do. Was it worth a trade?

He always lost. We laid out his right arm on the bed and flopped over his hand on its back, palm up. He could barely move any of his fingers except the first one. When we came into these sessions, he tried his best to cheat by making it look as if he was moving his fingers when he flexed his palm a bit. Ever since the first time I caught him doing this, I had been hard on him. I also threatened to penalize him 15 moves for cheating.

After all this baloney, we got down to the hard stuff. I took a hold of his last three fingers with one hand, his thumb with my other hand, and then with his hand flat on the pillow, with his first finger free, I would look him square in the eye and dare him, "Go ahead, move that finger."

Always the same thing. A big deep breath, a tightening all over his body and then a strained face. He usually got a little redder in the face but no movement came to the finger.

"Ahhhhhhh," he would say as he let out his breath, "It must be my poor brain. I tell it to move my finger and it can't do it. I guess I've forgotten how. What needs working on is my poor brain."

"I know what you mean," I said, "I feel the same way about my legs and feet when I take a big breath and grunt and strain and don't get any movement. It's like I've lost some of my marbles."

That particular day, we tried it a little differently. We draped his hand over a little sandbag as I took hold of his fingers and thumb with both of my hands. The long breath, the tightening and then there it was. His finger was moving! Not much, but a little. I checked to see if he was doing it with his palm again.

I held his fingers tight and his thumb too. His finger was moving, not much, but back and forth it went. We both could see it. His smile captured his face as he let out his air this time without the "Ahhhhh." He had a happy face, happier than any other time since he first slept without the respirator. It was amazing how big something so small could be. Dennis was lifted up, soaring as on eagle's wings.

I could feel hope soaring in Dennis. Metch came in while Dennis was still resting after his great effort.

"I did it, Metch. I done did it."

"It sure took you a long time to get around to doing it," she chided Dennis, but her smile of pleasure and the gleam—like moisture—in her eyes said something else. She had yet another reward to help balance all the heartaches. "You wouldn't be fooling me now, would you?"

"I did it. Ask Bob if you don't believe me."

"He did it, Metch."

"Let's see."

"Ok, Bob, come on, let's show her."

We set up again. The long breath came, only naturally, nothing happened. He tried twice, and then, exhausted, he said, "You wait, Metch, I'll show you."

He was disappointed he couldn't show Metch, but he knew he had done it.

"That's okay, Metch, I know I did it."

That night, as Dennis and I read the newspaper, we were actually able to share the paper a little. Dennis could now hold one page in his left hand. He said he could read the paper this way, but the shaking left some doubt. Headlines, yes, he could make those out, but he was lying about the regular print.

Abruptly, he stopped and listened. He heard it before the rest of us did because he had been there before. We listened to the new patient going into the room across the hall from us. There was much activity there. Nurses coming and going quickly. Feet shuffling, wheels squeaking on machines as they were rolled in. And then we heard the weak cough. It was dry as when Rick first began to pump on Dennis' chest. The cough was repeated because it wasn't accomplishing anything. The cough was like a magnet, pulling us right into the hell in that room. "That's bad over there," winced Dennis.

The patient was a pretty blond woman of 26, mother of three children. Five days earlier, her twin sister had been in the same room with bulbar polio. She died very quickly in the typical spectacular way of bulbar. She left four children motherless.

The twin in there now also had bulbar. Somehow she knew she had the same thing her sister had had and she was scared to death. Fear surrounded her. She saw what had happened to her sister in the same room and now she was taking the same course. Bed tilted up in the air, head down and oxygen bubbling life into her through the green tube in her nose.

The night shift came on and the quiet of the night accentuated the activity and sounds in her room. We could hear distinctly what was going on over there. The coughing became weaker. After gargling on her phlegm for a while, she began to choke. We cleared our own throats.

Enter the suction machine to do its efficient work. The long chrome nozzle, slightly bent to fit the throat, gleamed at the end of the long red rubber hose. Sliding down her all but collapsed throat, the suction machine slurped the mucous and phlegm from out of her windpipe. Dennis winced again as he heard the distinct sound of that machine when it hissed and slurped. He had been there. He knew how hideous the machine was at doing its work.

"Sometimes, if its aim is bad, it feels like part of your guts are being sucked up."

To me, the suction machine sounded hungry. It almost made me gag. Both Dennis and I knew it was going to be a long, long night. And it was not long before she began to cry out in a faint voice, "Help. Oh, please, won't someone help me? Please help me. Please."

No one could really help her. She was going this one all by herself except for a few pieces of equipment. At the moment, it was the suction machine. Just the fact that it was being used was a bad sign.

We traced the progress of the bulbar's attack at the base of her brain as the throat muscles collapsed. Her attempt to breathe, her dry coughs and the suction machine's hisses all became a conglomeration of sputtering sounds that made my stomach squirm and my heart ache.

Morning came, and she was doing poorly. She no longer knew what was going on. She called out, saying, "There's a message from my doctor at the front desk giving me permission to go home. I want to go home. My doctor has released me."

She knew just one thing. She wanted to get away from all the awful things associated with polio—the machines, the pain and the fear of knowing what had happened to her sister. It would have been nice if she could have been released, leaving all behind including the bulbar.

Of course the opposite was true; it had a fixed death grip on her. As morning passed, her throat muscles were entirely gone and her breathing was cut off. Her strength was sapped from the battle through the night. To alleviate her suffocating, her doctor was forced to perform a tracheotomy. He cut her throat just below the Adam's apple and inserted an oxygen tube that reached the lungs, bringing its life-giving bubbles. That kept her alive even though she couldn't breathe. It gave her relief but it didn't stop the bulbar. The tracheotomy was another bad sign, worse than the suction machine. It almost always said, "Bad things are in store shortly."

She went quickly; by afternoon, she was in the iron lung and she died the next morning. Then followed the sickening smell of the disinfectant in the room, and it was all over. The room was quiet, ready for the next patient. Twin sisters in a week.

Both Dennis and I were glad Johnny wasn't in with us any longer. He would probably have asked some questions we certainly couldn't have answered. There wasn't any reason. It was just because. . . . Why?

CHAPTER SEVEN

Bobby, Baths and Bedlam

Life went on in the midst of tragedy on the polio floor. There were signs of improvement and hope. Dennis and I were both better. He was up quite a bit in his wheelchair and I was taking my first shaky steps. I was having a little bit of feeling coming into my feet. I could have walked more if an aide on each side had been there to steady me, but we were still short of help.

There were more changes. Bobby was moved in with us. He had graduated from the iron lung room. He was the one I told Johnny about. The bulbar patient who was almost a miracle if he wasn't one already. I was wrong in thinking he was only a bit older than Johnny. Bobby was ten, but small for his age.

He was much quieter than Johnny, but he had one outstanding characteristic. He was constantly hungry. What he wanted to eat was about five or six Harket's cheeseburgers, but he couldn't have them because his throat was still too sore and weak. He did manage to scrounge all the food Dennis and I didn't eat. The right side of his face was still affected by muscle spasms and, to some extent, was paralyzed. The result was that he seemed to be constantly winking. This provided a certain amount of amusement for Dennis and me.

"Bobby, stop winking at me," was my observation, "I'll bet you wink at all the girls now, don't you?"

"No, I don't because if I did, I would get my face slapped."

"Well, Bobby, there are some girls who would slap your face for winking at them, but there are others who wouldn't mind at all."

"Yah? Well suppose you show me the difference?"

I did not expect this kind of an answer, and suddenly felt a bit defensive. This feeling increased as I looked up to see Hillard and Norall standing in the doorway listening to our conversation. Bobby had me on the spot as they remained to hear my answer.

"Ah, you wouldn't understand," was my weak reply. "I'll tell you later."

Dennis and I soon found that we couldn't steamroll over Bobby the way we did Johnny when it came time to listen to our usual evening menu of detective and horror stories on the radio. We couldn't draw him in by suggesting he try them to see what they were like.

"Those programs are trash. My mom says so. I listened to one once, and she's right. I want good music on at night. That's what we listen to at home. There's some good music on at night."

Back home was a farm out in the Platte Valley where the soil was apt to be sandy and good crops hard to come by except in wet years. Bobby's parents were both hard workers on the farm. Whatever profit they made went back into the farm to pay for machinery, seed, or the mortgage. Not much was left over for some of the nicer things in life that many of us enjoyed and usually took pretty much for granted.

Dennis and I had picked up this much about Bobby by listening to him and his parents when they came to visit. So a change took place, and we accepted Bobby's idea for evening radio. We both enjoyed the music Bobby recommended. That seemed to please him, so he told us more about his home life.

"Dad put in our first indoor toilet last fall. It's really nice, back of the kitchen where the big closet used to be. That was a big thing for Mom. Had a lot to do with communicating."

"Communicating? A toilet has a lot to do with communicating?" I asked, more than just a bit puzzled. I am sure my curiosity came through in my voice as well.

"Yep, it all has to do with speaking what's on your mind. But more than that, though, it also has a lot to do with listening. Mostly though, it has to do with getting your idea across to the other person. We've all been working on this idea back home, particularly Dad."

Bobby certainly had our attention. I had a hard time believing I was hearing this from him, but I also had the feeling I was about to learn something out of the ordinary.

"Can you give us an example of what you mean, Bobby?"

The bright look on his face said he was ready for us.

"If I want something, and I tell you I want it or need it and you don't listen, then I have to do something to get you to hear me like saying, 'Bob, you didn't hear me about those evening radio programs, did you?'"

Even Dennis sat up a bit straighter at that. "That's really very good. Bobby, where did you get all this?"

"At home. We've been practicing on it ever since Mom came home last fall from the hospital. Our doctor has been helping Mom and Dad in group meetings and I even went to one of those meetings once."

We were getting into a very personal area of Bobby's life with his parents, but I didn't want to shut him off either.

"Sounds to me as if you've learned your communication lesson very well. That's really good."

"That's kinda what Dad said when he found out what Mom wanted. Yep, that's when he built her the toilet in the house. Up to then, we just had a biffy out back."

"You mean your mom asked your dad to build an indoor toilet, and he did?"

"Yes, he did, but not till after Mom got sick and was in the hospital for a spell. Dad said it was nerves. After she came home, Mom and Dad started going to those meetings. They were supposed to help them learn how to communicate and understand each other.

"Mom said she knew Dad had to put all our money back into the farm so we can build it up. We hope to be more like the rich people some day. But Mom told the doctor that somewhere in the middle of all that hard work, she and Dad lost something. That's when their communications broke down. Mom just felt that Dad didn't care any more."

"Oh it's better now between your mom and dad?" I said in a rather small voice.

"It sure is, now that Dad has put in the toilet. I really like using it, particularly this past winter. Don't have to go outside in the cold anymore.

"But you know, the toilet stands for something between Mom and Dad. I figured that out all by myself. You see, Mom asked Dad lots of times to put the toilet in, but he never did. Not even in the winter time when he might have had the time. After a while, like maybe a year, his not putting it in became a sign to Mom that he didn't care about her anymore. It was a sign to her that he didn't love her anymore. And that hurt Mom real bad. She got sick from it.

"Course that wasn't true at all. Dad really did love Mom, only he didn't know how to communicate it so good."

The way Bobby said "communicate" told me that he had been practicing saying the word as well as working on what it meant.

"Mom told me all about it the day that Dad found out."

"Found out?" repeated Dennis with an obvious question in his head.

"Yep. When Dad found out what the toilet meant to Mom, or what his not putting in the toilet meant to her. They were in a group meeting, talking like they do every week. The time I went the people all talked about their feelings. Kinda dumb not being able to say how you feel about something or what you mean. I don't know, it's all deep down grown-up stuff.

"Anyway, they were talking, and this one man in the group, not the doctor, got to talking to Mom and Dad about the toilet. Somehow, the man said to Mom and Dad, 'You mean, Jim's not building your toilet after you asked him so many times became a sign to you that he quit loving you?'

"Mom said she just hung her head down and nodded it hurt so much to talk about it. But that's when Dad finally heard what it was all about. That's when the communication finally got working.

"Mom says, Dad jumped up all of a sudden, not knowing what to do as he stared down at the floor for a while. And then he turned to her and said, 'Well, let's get out of here!'

"And he grabbed her by the right wrist and darn near pulled her off her feet he went out the door so fast. That's what Mom says. The toilet got built the next day and we've all been working on communicating ever since. And Mom and Dad never did go back to another of those meetings."

After Bobby finished, it grew quiet in the ward and it remained that way for quite a while. I wonder how far away Dennis and I were in our thoughts after listening to Bobby.

There was no doubt that Bobby was special to us after that. Special in a new way. I experienced an extra fine feeling inside when his parents came to visit. I think I understood a little why Bobby had been spared the ferocity of the bulbar. He had a beautiful message to communicate and so did his mom and dad.

Other growing signs: Dennis was going to his bath in a wheelchair and I was getting so I could almost give myself my own bath. I could really do it without any assistance. But there came a Saturday morning when the PT wasn't there, and we were unusually short of help.

"Sure, I can give myself a bath," I replied when asked if I could. "I can just wheel down there and pull myself up and into the tub without any trouble at all."

At the bath, I drew the water, but I failed to realize that my polio had reduced my sensitivity to the heat of the water in my left hand and arm. I used my left hand to test the temperature of the water as being okay, and then I heaved myself up and over the edge of the tub to relax in the water. I floated with the back of my head on a pad. But once in the water, it wasn't long before I realized I had made the bath water too hot. I became dizzy and limp as nausea surged through me. And then a most frightening event struck me. I went blind! I couldn't see! Hundreds of white pin prick dots danced before me and I felt as though I was losing my breath.

In desperation, I cried out, "Help! Help! Somebody get me out of this tub. Something terrible is happening to me. I can't see. I can't breathe! Get me out of here!"

At that point, I was half out of the tub. I was feeling down into space for my wheelchair like a blind person. I could have fallen. Suddenly a firm hand took me by my shoulder and under the armpit. "You're all right," said a strange voice.

He swung me into my wheelchair and off we went. I told him which ward I was in. As we came into the ward, he called out, "He's had some kind of accident in the tub. Which is his bed?"

I heard Mother on the ward and she showed him my bed. I told Mother, "I got the water too hot. Had some kind of heat stroke. Can't see anything except all kinds of white dots going round and round."

By then, I was on my bed and my heart wasn't pounding so hard anymore and I could begin to see. Was I ever glad to see again! As I rested in bed, much of the weakness passed but I stayed in bed for the rest of the day. I was terribly frightened. I waited until the next day to continue my therapy.

At lunch the next day, I looked up to see Dennis calmly pushing a fork into his mouth all by himself. Rick was looking on in amazement. Another milestone. A simple event in everyday life was a big milestone for Dennis in his recovery. His first forkful of food put into his own mouth all by himself. He tried again. Success a second time! But the third time, his left arm was exhausted and the fork fell from his hand half way up.

Within a week, he did a whole meal by himself, but that was an exceptional day. For the moment, he was happy yet one more time on his road to complete recovery. "Maybe he'll end up stronger than before he had polio," was my thought.

Labor Day found us still in the hospital. I had been there more than a month. We listened to the radio warnings about how to take safe swimming precautions and how to follow safe driving procedures. There was the dire prediction of how many traffic deaths would occur over that three-day holiday weekend. Dennis was amused by those warnings as he contemplated our situation.

"You know, Bob, this is one time we've got them all fooled. We've got it made. We are in the safest place there can be for this weekend. It isn't everyone who can be as fortunate as we are!"

The humor of this caused him to laugh, which he couldn't do very well. Doctor's orders were, "No laughing," but Dennis couldn't help it that time.

"Yes sir, Bob, I really am fortunate to be so safe, but I really wouldn't mind being just a little bit reckless. That's if I could be."

As we listened to the news of the traffic deaths on the nation's highways, the irony of our situation hit home. We were safe. Some of those not so safe soon joined us downstairs in the emergency room. Our hospital was the receiving hospital for all the police reported traffic accidents in the metropolitan area. Ambulances came with their sirens wailing.

As the three days went on, more members of our staff left the floor to assist in helping with the carnage the ambulances were bringing in.

On Sunday night, Rick came in shaking his head, "We had two attempted suicides, three drunk drivers near death, and a near drowning victim. Down there it seems like the people want to throw away their lives, but we're saving them. While up here, people are fighting to live, and we're losing too many. It doesn't make any sense."

"No reason," said Dennis.

But following the death of the second twin mother, it did seem as though the violence of the polio was slackening off. There were more cases, but none seemed to be nearly so bad as many of the earlier ones were. Perhaps the polio was being diagnosed in time now or whatever, but the wards were getting full to overflowing. We were receiving more children from the overflow at Children's Hospital.

A lieutenant colonel from SAC headquarters came in with both legs out and found himself in the isolation ward with a bunch of screaming kids. He couldn't wait until his isolation period was up. In the meantime, he could hardly stand the situation. Somehow, to me, a private in the army at the end of the war, his situation seemed to have some poetic justice built in. Who says polio was all bad? The nurses told me the kids didn't understand the colonel when he screams at them to "Be at ease!" Looked like he was in for some basic training.

A day or two after Labor Day, Dennis was given the "go ahead" to be transferred to a hospital in Kansas City so he could be closer to his family at St. Joseph, Missouri. He was excited and ready to

go. We all knew it and were excited for him. Then came what seemed
to be the last straw. He had to wait about a week before a bed could
be cleared for him! It seemed to me the long wait was cruel. He had
waited so long. Had I been in his shoes, and I was glad I was not, I
don't think I could have remained very calm. I'd probably be uptight. But not Dennis. It was just a few days more for him.

He had learned well his lesson of patience. Learned it much
better than I had. In 75 days, he had grown so strong in so many
ways, and, in those 75 days, it seemed to me he had lived a thousand
years, patiently!

As he waited for the bed to clear in Kansas City, Dennis began
to do some frisky things, probably just to keep up his spirits. Or
perhaps it was an outlet for his pent-up happiness at seeing the end
in sight. The radio was playing some Glen Miller music as he called
out, "Hey, I used to be a pretty good dancer in my time, how about
this one?"

I felt uneasy as he did a fancy little two-step at the end of his
bed as he held his arms close across his chest, holding the bad right
arm with the better left arm. His eyes were closed. No telling who
he thought was in his arms.

"Now watch this," he called as he did another step with a swirl
at the end. Rick came in. He too was obviously uncomfortable as
he moved up to Dennis. But Rick was too late.

The fall came at the end of the swirl as Dennis had a big smile
on his face. The smile turned to terror as he toppled right into his
wheelchair. My breath went short. Rick was on him in an instant.
It seemed as if it took forever for Rick to turn him over and out of
his heap in the wheelchair. It was very quiet. Rick sat Dennis up
in the wheelchair to have a look at him. It was an anxious moment.
Then Dennis smiled one more time.

He was all right! A little battered, but he was not hurt. As a
matter of fact, his fall turned out to be a blessing. He did his fall
well, rolling right into the wheelchair the easy way with a little fade
away to avoid the crash. Really well done. Here he was, able to improve his confidence in one more way.

It was almost as if he had some kind of guardian angel working
around him. I could almost feel its force but I didn't say anything
about it because I didn't understand it. Now, he was learning how
to fall well. Do a good fall. I made a point to remember that caper,
it might come in handy for me some day. The key to falling was to
relax and not tighten up.

CHAPTER EIGHT

Can't Communicate

Events began to take place quickly. I was released from the hospital a few days before Dennis finally went to Kansas City. But I had to come back to the hospital every afternoon for PT treatments as an out-patient. Two days before I was released, we received a fourteen-year-old boy in with bulbar. It looked bad right from the start. He was in the iron lung room for special treatment.

Getting out of the hospital was quite an experience for me. I more or less expected to walk out of the place as I had been walking around the ward a few steps in my slippers the last few days. There were some surprises for me. Simply putting on my shoes turned out to be an enormous effort.

They felt as though each weighed about fifteen pounds. By the time I was dressed, I was worn out. I went out in a wheelchair and was glad to have it. I went out on Sunday and came back on Monday for therapy. When I came back on Monday, there was a good chance I would stay, I was so shaky. I rode some in the wheelchair but tried walking into the hospital. I settled for the wheelchair.

As I went by the iron lung room, I saw the boy with the bulbar in there. His neck was swathed with a bandage and a long thin red tube was sticking down to an oxygen tank.

"He had a tracheotomy during the night and he almost died," Metch told me. "His parents and a priest were here most of the night. But he seems to be rallying. He just might make it. You know how it is with bulbar, the longer you stay alive, the more chance there is for making it, like Bobby did. When it kills, bulbar kills pretty quickly, as you know."

After therapy, I stopped to see Dennis. He was lonely and a bit on the sad side just waiting to go to Kansas City. How he wanted to get on that plane! I brought him a couple of cigars and we rehashed "Life with Luigi" from the radio the night before, but it went over like a steel cloud. We soon fell silent but Bobby started talking about the boy with bulbar.

"I hope he makes it. It sure is scary, being in that room with the lights and the machines. It's like you're way inside yourself and then again you're not. People are working on you and you hardly know what you can do and what you can't. What you're doing and what you aren't. At first, it's a terrible feeling, finding out you can't breathe on your own and that the oxygen going down the tube from the tracheotomy is doing it for you. After a while I could relax a little but it was weird. It was the phlegm coming up my collapsed throat that was the most scary.

"Lying in the bed tilted up in the air with my head down was spooky enough, but that phlegm coming up was awful. I felt like I was going to choke all the time as I could feel it sliding up to my mouth. It gets so frightening, that sometimes I felt like a frightened little bird crouched down over in the corner of the room looking on at myself with everyone working on me. I remember feeling so cold and alone, like no one knew how I felt."

Bobby didn't talk very much, but when he did, it was usually well worth listening to. And when he finished, it usually was quiet in the ward for a while as it was this time. He seemed to unlock some heavy thoughts inside each of us.

On my way out of the hospital, I stopped to look into the lung room again. Norall was there working with the suction machine again, and as she finished, the boy rolled over on his side toward me. The oxygen continued to bubble down the little red tube and yet his mouth was open as though he was trying to breathe. I thought of what Bobby said and shuddered. Maybe he didn't know what was going on or then perhaps he thought he was a frightened little bird over in the corner too. It was pathetic seeing him trying to breathe, trying to make the effort. He hadn't learned to relax yet with the bubbles going down the red tube bringing life to him.

I wondered if he did know what it was all about. From the set expression on his face and the look in his eyes—and I could see mile after mile into those eyes—I could tell he was a fighter. He was squared away for the biggest fight of his life. I wanted to tell him I was pulling for him.

Life on the outside wasn't going so well for me. My left leg was much weaker than when I left the hospital. The progressive nature of polio was still at work. It scared me to see myself going backwards in recovery, but if I felt sorry for myself for a moment, all I had to do was think of the boy with bulbar.

Back at the hotel where I was staying, Mother was trying to help me do things but I felt her hovering over me again. It made me nervous. I knew she meant well. The setting probably had something to do with my anxiety. The hotel was near the hospital so Mother could get me back and forth for therapy, but it was far from being an attractive place. Lots of older people around.

The next day, as I came down the hall to the PT room, I noticed the lung wasn't in the hall where it usually was kept. As I went by the lung room, I saw the boy was in it. When I stopped to see Dennis, he told me the events of the night.

"They thought he was going in the middle of the night. His parents and the priest came again. Somehow, he made it one more time but no one knows really how he did it. He's got a lot of guts, that kid. But it was too much for his mother last night and she fainted.

"I had fallen off to sleep but was awakened by a disturbance on the ward in the middle of the night. I looked down to the foot of the bed where you had been next to me, and there was a priest standing there. And at the foot of the bed, there was a pair of women's feet.

"I just couldn't figure out what the score was, for the priest was mumbling. The thing gave me a jolt. Rick came in after a bit and told me they had brought in the mother to rest after she had fainted. She was resting in the bed next to me. It must have been rough on all of them. I hope the kid makes it."

"It doesn't look good," said Bobby. "But I think he'll make it. He's a fighter."

So he hadn't gone. Somehow, he had rallied for the second time. He just wouldn't give up the fight. So far, he had taken about all the bulbar could throw at him and he was holding his own. Might even have been a bit stronger. He looked to me as if he were going to make it. I felt he would. Bobby thought so too.

That afternoon, a much younger boy was in the lung room too. He was another bulbar case. His condition was poor. He had recently had the mumps right after getting over scarlet fever. Now he had polio. There wasn't much left in him to fight the bulbar. I could hear it rattling in his throat as I went down the hall on my way out.

My doctor called me at the hotel to say he didn't think I was making much progress in my out-patient therapy program at the hospital. I told him I thought I was going backward. He wanted me to go to the Veterans Hospital in Lincoln. That was where Ed was. There was supposed to be good therapy there. I thought that was a good move. During the week I had been living at the hotel, my left leg had become much weaker.

My right knee no longer locked regularly, so I was subject to falls at any time. I still had no feeling to speak of in my feet. Fortunately, I had been able to catch myself on furniture in my room most of the time when my knee gave out, but I had one nasty fall and I bruised some ribs. I relied more and more on my wheelchair. It was safer. I knew I felt very insecure with living at the hotel and going to the hospital for therapy. It was like being in a pit and not being able to get out.

I called the V.A. Hospital at Lincoln and the administrator said I could come at the end of the week. I felt good about that move as it would take the pressure off Mother at the hotel. She was trying to be my nurse, and she simply couldn't make it. I couldn't make it. She wasn't up to it, and I thought we both needed some space for me to be able to recover. I looked forward to the change.

When I got off the elevator at the hospital for my afternoon therapy, I was stopped cold by the sickening odor of the disinfectant. For a moment, I was stunned cold. I did not want to go down the hall past the iron lung room for my therapy.

"It could be the younger boy," I thought to myself. "He was in such poor shape yesterday afternoon."

I was wrong. The iron lung was out in the hall again. This meant it was the fourteen-year-old. I was wrong again. Both of them had died that morning. I felt sick. I looked around—at the iron lung, at the rooms, and down the hall. The ball in my stomach grew heavier. I was glad I was out of that place. I was glad I was going to the hospital at Lincoln. I needed to get away from that place with all the tragedy.

I stopped to see Dennis. He was gone. I looked at his empty bed in disbelief. At first, I felt a great loss, and I felt it in the pit of my stomach. And then, even in the gloom of that place, a smile worked its way across my face. I grinned.

"He made it! He finally made it and got out of this place. This is great! Here is something to feel good about. I feel like shouting!"

Metch was on the floor and she told me about the morning. "He left here about ten this morning. Happiness was all over his face. He looked real good. He said to say 'good-bye' to you. I shall miss him terribly. We went through so much together from the very beginning right up to this morning.

"He was so sick and yet he was always so strong in spirit. He is such a class guy. He gives so much to all of us. He's a rare individual with such a rare combination of patience and strength. His outlook on life is healthy, it simply overflows to the rest of us. He has everything going for him. There is so much hope for his parents. That is more than I can say about the parents of the two boys we lost this morning."

I could see that Metch was about wrung out emotionally as she continued.

"The younger boy never was in it. His plug had been pulled before he got here from fighting the mumps and scarlet fever. I think we all knew that. He died almost without a whimper. But the fourteen-year-old, he gave it such a battle. After we put him in the iron lung yesterday, he seemed to rally. He got in rhythm with the lung right away and let it do his breathing for him. He didn't fight it the way some people do. Maybe we should have put him in the lung sooner. We never know.

"The tracheotomy was holding and by last night, he seemed stronger. And he was so determined to live! He and I were a team, working together much as Dennis and I did. I could feel him getting stronger. I would do something for him and he would nod his head a little or blink his eyes a touch to let me know he was with me. He was going to beat that bulbar.

"Then last night, his skin began to shrivel up. That meant just one thing. His heart was going. His messages couldn't get through to his heart anymore. His heart got so it didn't know what to do. We were helpless. There was nothing we could do. He gave it all he had before he died. He never gave up thinking he could make it.

"Hillard says he fought harder and longer against the bulbar than any other patient we've had this year. Fought even harder against the bulbar than Bobby and that's saying mountains. He should have lived. I don't understand it. I just don't understand it."

Metch gave herself the luxury of a few tears before she went on. I looked down at my feet. I could feel her grief. It was mine too, but I didn't know how to cry as she did.

"The little boy's blood was so bad when he came in, the doctor was afraid to do a tracheotomy even though he needed it. But the bulbar took charge and made the decision for the doctor. It soon became apparent that it was a tracheotomy or else. The kid died on the operating table."

Two in one day. I was glad to be out of there. I was glad to have my change coming. But I could never really get away from that hospital. There was too much of me and Dennis and Metch and Bobby and Johnny and all the rest in that place. That night there was a small article in the newspaper saying that two more polio victims died at County Hospital.

Not much connection between that simple statement and what I knew. Not much communication there, but how could anyone understand who hadn't been there?

On my last day at the hospital, Metch handed me an envelope addressed to me at the hospital. Inside was a "get well" card. Inside the card below the message was a very scratchy but clear signature. It was from Dennis!

PART II
The Eye of the Storm

CHAPTER NINE

More Than My Plan

The ten days I spent at the Colonial Hotel in Omaha were pivotal in my life. Going to and from the hospital for the out-patient therapy each day took a long two hours. The rest of the time I was at the hotel, and I was incredibly bored. I came into a bad attitude. Depressed over not making progress, I didn't know what to do with myself in that drab hotel room. Maybe I had already become institutionalized in the six weeks I had been in the hospital. Maybe that's why I couldn't get a positive attitude going. I probably didn't know I was dependent on the system, and now it wasn't there. Whatever it was, I was hard to get along with.

"Leave me alone! I can do it myself." I don't know how many times I snapped this at Mother as I tried to get around in the hotel room. If it was going to be done, I was going to do it. I tried pulling on my pants one time, got my feet twisted in them and fell heavily to the floor. I just missed, by less than an inch, bashing my head against the radiator. I didn't say to myself, "You were lucky," but I was able to scream at Mother often in my anger. She was hearing a very big "I" and an equally strong will expressed in my anger.

I can never ever recall praying during this entire experience with polio. Never once did I ask God to help me. Never once did I thank Him. I was going this one all by myself, and more loneliness and agony were going along inside of me than I cared to realize. The pain of my polio experience had laid bare feelings that were ready for healing, but I didn't know how to ask for healing. I didn't know I needed healing of feeling feelings. I only knew I was trying to get back feelings in my legs and wanted to walk again.

I knew I was a survivor, and I knew I had a very strong will. What I didn't know was that I was an Adult Child of an Alcoholic and that I had adopted a role in life as a rescuer. The drunken behavior of my father, whom I dearly loved, had led me to shut off my feelings completely. I found that having them was too expensive, so I turned to rescuing to cover up dealing with them.

As a boy, I had done very well at rescuing both my father and then my mother, but right now I couldn't seem to rescue me. Since I didn't know God, and I had to rely solely on my own plan, my plan was badly bent in the shape of two weak and fumbling legs. I couldn't have articulated all of this then, but at least I was aware that anger was running the show. Eventually, my polio experience was going to show me how to deal with the "feelings" disease of family alcoholism.

At the moment, my pride was shutting down my practice of patience the way Dennis had taught me how to do it. And my self-pity bag was stifling me from relying on courage the way Bobby had. Right then, I simply didn't have any peace or serenity to draw on. I was truly out of sorts, and the frustration and anger were the reality of my life. Some life. I just couldn't see how anything was going to fit and make sense.

When Mother came back from California to take her position as nurse's aide at the hospital, she was able to come back to Omaha because an old friend, away for the summer, had offered Mother her apartment. That helped her make ends meet financially so she could take the job at the hospital and be near me.

While living in that apartment, she became acquainted with a woman, Mrs. Melinda Lockwood, living in an apartment on the floor below. Mrs. Lockwood heard that I was bored and was looking for something to do. Her response was to give Mother her typewriter for me to have. Just like that, out of the kindness of her heart, she gave me her typewriter, and she didn't even know me.

I had a hard time believing the story about Mrs. Lockwood and her typewriter, but once it sank in, I felt overwhelmed by her kindness. I sat down to write her a "thank you" note on her green typewriter. In the process, I told her some things about Dennis. Then I heard that she had shown my letter to a friend. The friend was moved by my account of Dennis to give $150 to the National Foundation for Infantile Paralysis.

That was a lot of money! It sparked an idea in my head.

"Holy smokes," I thought. "I wonder if I could write more about my polio experience. It might do some good. I've never written anything to speak of, except term papers and my thesis. This is a whole new area. I'll see what I can do."

Suddenly, I had some purpose to my life, and my anger found some positive expression. I was revving up inside. I could feel it. So I set out to write my story about polio in the County Hospital at Omaha. The story, as it is written up to this point, is what I wrote on the green typewriter during those ten days in that hotel room.

Mrs. Carpenter, the woman who gave the money, also gave me a present. It was a beautiful leather bound Bible with her name printed on the cover in gold, "Mrs. I. W. Carpenter." I didn't use that Bible for a long time. It had no meaning to me then. But then, neither the Bible nor God had any place in my life.

Writing the polio account kept me busy and away from dealing with my deeper feelings that were trying to get out. For instance, I was totally incapable of saying, "I am getting more and more anxious about what is going to happen to me as my out-patient therapy deteriorates. What kind of a plan will work? What will I do for money? I am totally broke, and the National Foundation has paid over $300.00 of my hospital bill."

There was absolutely no peace working in me during those ten days at the hotel. I really did not have any place to go other than the V.A. hospital at Lincoln. I felt battered. I wanted to be cheerful over my move to Lincoln, but I was close to being desperate. I didn't know what was left in the polio storm for me, but I did know that the peace in the eye of the storm was a false peace.

PART III
Stormy and Clearing

CHAPTER TEN

V.A. Hospital, and Zim

When I went to the V.A. Hospital at Lincoln, I went with certain expectations and preconceived ideas about what the place would be like. I expected my stay there to be something like being in a nursing home, a place where I would live a relaxed kind of life, gaining back my strength. I would do some exercises, read a lot and maybe continue to write.

I knew where the V.A. Hospital was. We used to drive by it on our way to the Nebraska Cornhusker football games. We often sat in the east stands up in the balcony; from there I could see the hospital. From far back into my childhood, I can remember seeing it this way. Dad would point it out as we drove by and say, "That's the Veterans Hospital. That's the place I could go if I didn't have money enough to go to a regular hospital."

My father had served in the Army during World War I, and we all knew he was eligible to go to the V.A. Hospital if he wanted to when he had his hernia operation. But even during the Depression when we were piling up huge bills he didn't pay, Dad didn't choose to go to the V.A. Hospital. So his remarks had colored my thinking. Going to the V.A. Hospital had been beneath him, even during those bleak days of the Depression. That's what I remembered most about driving by that big red brick building set far back from the street. It had white trim and was supposed to look colonial in its style of architecture.

I did not expect a very high level of care or competency. I was in for a surprise. My aunt and uncle drove me to the hospital. Mother came too. I had all my stuff with me, including my radio and books.

At the receptionist's desk, I received a rude awakening. No radios allowed. Each bed had a headset with earphones plugged into a wall plug offering four local stations. No books. No typewriters either. As a matter of fact, all I could bring in was one suitcase, my cane, and then they made an exception, I could bring in my briefcase too.

It was quite a scene with my family lugging all my stuff in by the armful and then my being denied entrance with any of it except just the bare essentials. I looked at my uncle, half expecting him to say or do something so I could take my stuff in. I think he looked at me, expecting me to do the same. I know we looked out of place. A young man in a wheelchair off to the side was taking all of this in.

I felt uneasy by this display of regimentation. I said good-bye to my aunt and uncle and to Mother. I was taken in a wheelchair to my bed in a small six-bed ward, which was on the first floor at the end of the south wing of the hospital.

Across the hall was another small ward like the one I was in, and at the end of our wing was a bright, sunny sunporch with all kinds of equipment for the polio patients. Five of the six beds in my ward were empty. Mac, another polio patient, was lying on his bed, trying to do some of his morning exercises. He paused to observe my arrival. He had to work hard not to snicker at me. He told me later, "You sure looked like a dude coming into our humble ward. You with your briefcase, and all dressed up in a coat and tie. You looked as if we weren't up to your level. It didn't make me feel mad particularly, just kind of curious."

My grand arrival was one thing the group didn't let me forget for a while. The young man in the wheelchair at the entrance turned out to be George Malnack, known as Russian, another one of my fellow patients from the ward across the hall. He thoroughly enjoyed telling how I had arrived at the entrance desk with all my junk in hand. Russian said, "He was dressed up like he was going to the Ritz, only you could tell by the look on his face that we didn't look like the Ritz to him."

After these chiding comments from Russian and Mac, it took me awhile to settle in with the group.

There were eight polio patients at that time in the two wards. Frey, a stroke victim, was with us for a while later on, but most of the time, the two wards with six beds each at the end of the first floor south wing were occupied only by polio patients. Mac did not stay with us long. He was an irrigation farmer from western Nebraska, and because of his concern for the upkeep of his farming operation, he went home before his time of recovery was anywhere nearly complete. He went home with a tremendous limp to his left leg. He was tall and angular, and his left hip almost shot out of its socket when he walked. I thought he left far too early, but he had his worries to deal with. He was a most positive person. I counted him as a true friend.

I was very tired by the time I reached my bed and sank down on it to rest. It was a hard bed. I asked Mac what made the bed so hard.

"A board," was his reply. "They put boards under all of our beds so we can do our bed exercises on a firm surface. It's Zim's idea. He says firm beds are good for our posture so the boards are a good idea."

"Who is Zim?" I inquired.

"He's the PT here at the hospital. You'll meet him directly."

And I did, most directly. I wandered out onto the sunporch in my wheelchair, following Mac after he finished his bed exercises. Just as we came out of our ward, another patient was wheeled into our ward, lying flat on a cart. He was pushed by a blond man in his late twenties—crew cut, square face, and obviously athletic.

"That's Zim," said Mac as we came out onto the sunporch.

What a nice place the sunporch was with mats for floor exercises. Later on I found out they were for wrestling too. Weights were on the wall to be pulled by those with weak arms. The weights could be increased or decreased according to our own choosing. Life size charts of muscles in colored drawings hung on the wall with names of the muscles clearly identified. In the corner of the sunporch, there was a long set of parallel bars with a full-length mirror at the end. I got out of my wheelchair and tried to walk between the bars as I watched in the mirror to see how I was doing. I wasn't doing very well; my left hip was flopping out badly.

"Hey, I want you to get back in your room and put your exercise suit on like the rest of the guys have." Zim barked at me as he came out on the sunporch, pushing the new patient. In his wheelchair, he looked stiff as a board.

"This here is Putzie. He's just come down from isolation and he's going to be in with you guys, Mac."

The new patient was a short German-looking man with a round face. Putzie was obviously most uncomfortable in his wheelchair. He was unable to sit up straight. He leaned way back and his legs stuck straight out over the foot guards of his wheelchair. His feet were rigid, at almost a 90-degree angle to his legs. He looked frightened. He was very stiff.

"What's wrong with them up on three?" snapped Zim. "They

should have been stretching you every day, Putzie, but they haven't. So now, we're going to have to get started like right now, and it will probably hurt."

By this time, I had found my way back into my wheelchair, and I was about to go to my bed to change into my exercise suit as Zim had ordered me, but now I was more interested in watching what Zim was doing. I was sitting just behind Putzie in my wheelchair when Zim sat down on the floor next to Putzie's right foot.

I quickly found out that Zim was a man of action. He placed his left hand at the back of Putzie's right ankle, and with his right hand he took the foot that was sticking up at right angles to the leg and firmly began to push the foot down at the toes. At the same time he pushed up on the ankle.

If Putzie had been stiff as a board up to this point, he instantly gave rigidity new meaning. Zim forced the foot down from its upright position. He was forcefully stretching Putzie's hamstrings by pushing the foot down, maybe even tearing them. I knew what it felt like but I had never been stretched the way Zim was stretching Putzie. The foot was going all the way down until it was going to be a natural straight continuation of the leg. Not once did Zim's pressure ease up. It was steady.

I could see beads of perspiration spring up on Putzie's forehead as he turned his head in pain. His deep draw for breath produced a faint whistle in his throat as the air rushed in. Then he screamed. I wonder how far the hair stood up on the back of my neck. I believe all 250 patients in our hospital heard Putzie's scream. Zim didn't stop for an instant until the foot was straight out. It was probably ten seconds. Putzie was sobbing and gasping for breath. His whole body was heaving. A look of hatred and disgust was on the Russian's face.

In his agony of deep gasps, Putzie spoke in a heavy whisper of jerky speech, "Zim, ... I know ... some day I'm going ... to thank you ... for what you are doing to me ... but right now ... if I could get my hands ... on you ... I'd kill you."

Not a single muscle moved or changed in the expression on Zim's face. He scooted across the floor on his butt until he reached Putzie's left leg. And of course then he did the same thing all over again to the left foot. Putzie screamed again even louder this time. He was sobbing. He was just a heap in his chair as I wheeled into my ward to change into my exercise suit. I felt sick to my stomach. I wondered what was in store for me at the hands of Zim. I soon found out when I came back out onto the sunporch.

"Your name's Bob? Bob, we have a routine of exercise for all the polio patients in the two wards. We have exercises on the beds and exercises out here on the sunporch. You will be given a schedule tomorrow morning when you go down to PT in the basement right after breakfast. You want to walk again. I want you to walk again. That's what I'm here for. I know what's best for you. I'm trained in physical therapy, and if we both work together, you will be completely healed and walking around like new. Okay?"

"Okay," I said.

"You can just work out here for the rest of the morning until lunch. After lunch and your rest period, Trudy will lead you for your afternoon occupational therapy out here on the sunporch. That's all her stuff down there at the other end."

When I looked at the other end of the sunporch to see what he was talking about, I saw a long bench with bars up high overhead arranged with straps hanging down. The straps were for holding up weak arms. There was a jigsaw next to the bench, only the power for the jigsaw came from pedals on a bicycle wheel down below. Next to the jigsaw was a grinder. It worked the same way the jigsaw worked; both were to be driven by weak legs pushing the pedals. Patients with weak legs pumped the jigsaw and grinder by pedaling the bicycle wheels, and patients with weak arms held the pieces of material to be cut by the saw and ground by the grinder.

The operation was designed as a real teamwork effort. Trudy's project turned out to be making sewing baskets out of clear plastic about three-eighths of an inch thick. All this therapy work was yet ahead of me, including weaving on the large floor loom next to the bench. There was going to be plenty of activity for me, but at the moment, I wanted to be very careful with Zim.

CHAPTER ELEVEN

Putzie and Onion

Zim pushed Putzie into our ward and helped him up on his bed. I followed them in as if to get something out of my night stand. After Zim left, I watched Putzie in obvious pain writhing back and forth across his bed. He was half whispering, "Oh, my God."

Another deep breath came as he turned his head to the wall, and again came the heavy whisper, "Oh, my God."

"That was pretty rough," I said.

"Yah, it still hurts, and I know I've got it coming again tomorrow, but I guess I've got to be stretched. Sure would be nice if it could be done some other way."

"I'm new here today. My name is Bob Hall. I'm from Omaha. Where are you from?"

"Pilger. I came in about three weeks ago. It's bad up on three. I'm glad to be down here even if I do have to be stretched by Zim. I'd sure like to have a beer."

"Did you ask for one?"

"Yah, but I can't have any."

"Why won't they give you a beer?"

"I've still got the catheter. They tell me no beer until they take that horseshit tube out of me. A beer sure would taste good right now. Might ease the pain."

"How long since you've had one?"

"Since the County Fair. The Wayne County Fair over three weeks ago. That's a long time for an Austrian to go without his beer. I came in from doing field work all afternoon so I could help the hired hand milk the cows. We were planning on doing the Fair after supper.

"I sat down to rest in the doorway of the barn where the step goes down into the milk parlor. It's a big step down. I can see over the tops of the cows waiting to be milked from there. I went to throw my left leg up to tie my boot, and 'whoops!' it hurt with a sharp pain in the small of my back and down into my legs. I didn't think much more about that sharp pain at the moment. Thought I was just tired. Dad has a big farm, and I had been putting in a lot of hours. You work hard in the summer. I remember my legs tightening up as I milked the cows. I was sitting on one of those three-legged milking stools. It was getting harder moving around, but me and the hired hand still went to the Fair anyway after supper.

"It was a chilly evening for early September, so I took my jacket along. I was glad I took it, because I began to have the chills, and it felt particularly good down in the small of my back where I was really getting tight. Even that last beer didn't taste very good to me, so I went home early.

"Next morning, I could hardly navigate. All I could do was sit on the floor after first sliding out of bed. After a while I felt strong enough to pull myself up by using the bottom of the bed, and I sort of hung on and rested. I could feel my right leg giving out whenever I tried to put any weight at all on it. My legs just began to give out, and I began to suspect polio. I wasn't afraid particularly, but I sure knew something was wrong. Really wrong.

"The doctor thought I had the lumbago. He wasn't sure what it was, so he gave me some sulfa and sent me home to take it easy in bed. The sulfa made me sick, and I threw up all over myself. I soon got worse. I got a lot worse, and I finally went to another doctor who gave me a spinal tap. I never had one of them before.

"When he gave it to me something went wrong because all of a sudden my left leg shot up out of my grasp in a funny way and just shook there all by itself. I wasn't doing a thing myself. As soon as the Doc seen that, he took the needle out and started all over again. The second time it went okay, but I began to have a bad feeling deep in my stomach. He said I had polio, and so they brought me down here. I was already so stiff, I just couldn't sit up. I was too tight. So I rode to Lincoln in an ambulance. I rode all the way in a lying down position, trying to rest and get comfortable. There was no way I could accomplish that. I was hurting too much. I went into isolation on the third floor as soon as I got here, and this is the first day I've been out. I'd sure like a beer."

Putzie put on his earphones, pulled the string to the wall jack a couple of times and tried to relax. Regular heavy breathing marked the arrival of sleep. I, too, found this was a good way to get a snooze in. Just lying in bed with the earphones on, listening to some easy music or in the afternoon to a baseball game, would put me to sleep in a short time.

At noon, I met some of the other patients when we went down to the cafeteria for lunch. On the way, I bumped into Ed. He was glad to see me and quickly shared some thoughts, "The chow here is really good. You go down the cafeteria line and just pick out what you want. They bring it to you at your table.

"At breakfast you can take juice or fruit, eggs or French toast. Sometimes pancakes, but their French toast is better. It depends on how hungry a person is. You can take rolls and toast and cereal, too. I like fresh fruit on my cereal. Same thing is true with lunch and dinner. It's good food."

If Ed was any indication of how good the food was, it had to be good. Obviously, he had gained some weight in the three weeks since I had seen him. He was still in his wheelchair, but he told me he was moving around a lot on Canadian sticks.

I didn't know what they were at first, so I asked him, and he explained, "They're light aluminum sticks, sort of like crutches that just come to your forearm. They have big wide bands that clamp around the outside of your forearm so you can lean against them, don't you know? Then there's a padded handle to grasp with your hand with the palm down so you can lean forward some. When you stand with them this way, you look a little like a gorilla standing up, leaning on his long forearms. I like the way they work.

"I take them right into the shower with me. Works slicker than a whistle. I had them take off the steel bottoms and put on extra large plastic bases. That's after I slipped a couple of times on the steel bottoms and then wore right through those little puny plastic caps. Got to get the extra large plastic bases. They work and they are holding up so far.

"There is a real art to walking with Canadian sticks. They work the way a stiff-legged doll works, don't you know? Got to get a push to get started, and then I swing my legs stiff legged out to the side and forward. You know, rock back and forth. Kinda get a rhythm going.

"Works particularly well for going up a hill or an incline. Once I get started, I don't want to stop. Gotta keep going to keep the swinging going. If I have to stop, I'm sunk. Awfully hard to get going again except on the level. I'm gaining confidence all the time. Takes a lot of hard work. When your legs aren't any good, you have to have good arms."

Then Ed said, "Have you seen those life-size muscle charts up on the sunporch?"

"Yah, I was looking at them this morning."

"It sure shows a fella how he can take a muscle and do something with it, even if there is just a little left. Or if you've completely lost a muscle, how you can make another take its place. I've learned a lot since coming here."

I told Ed about Putzie wanting his beer and not being able to have any. Ed snorted, "I've tried beer a couple of times since I've been here, and it just ruins me. I can't get close enough to a bathroom if I drink beer. Pity, too, because I love beer. Appreciate how Putzie feels. Too bad."

I tried going to lunch, pushing Ed in his wheelchair. I tried leaning on the handles as we went. It was farther than I thought and I was pooped by the time I got there. I was surely glad the servers at the cafeteria brought us our lunch after we picked it out. I had a ham sandwich, a bowl of tomato soup, a glass of milk, and some ice cream for dessert. It was good. The V.A. Hospital was looking up.

At the cafeteria, I noticed a number of men with their arms bound up in what looked like heavy splints. They were all going around holding their arms up high. I asked Ed what their trouble was.

"Corn picker got 'em all. Every last one. Those corn pickers are down-right greedy machines, particularly if you don't have the sense to turn one off. They're a fairly new machine on the farm. Since the end of the war, don't you know? We husked corn by hand up until last year. We'll probably see at least a dozen farmers going through the hospital this fall with their arms bound up in splints like that."

"What happens to them?" I asked.

"They try taking a short cut when the corn picker jams. They get down off their tractors and reach into the machines while they're still running. They think they can snatch away whatever it is that's jamming the pickers from working. Their glove or sleeve or even sometimes a strap from their overalls gets caught up in the chain, and in they go. You're seeing the lucky ones. Plenty of them will lose a whole arm. Have to have them amputated. What's left of them. Once in a while a farmer gets killed before the thing stops."

"Well, what are the splints for?"

"It's because of the surgery to pull the cut tendons back down. Those raised splints are a dead giveaway."

"Say," Ed said, changing the subject, "I didn't know you were a veteran. Where did you serve? You never talked it up much in Omaha."

"I was overseas in Kansas for 13 months right at the end of the war," I said with a sly smile. "I was chairborne paragrapher and had 50 missions to the PX."

That must not have sounded very interesting to Ed or any of the others. Most of them had been in the Pacific war and ended up in Japan after VJ Day. Ed didn't follow up on my reply. Instead, he introduced me to another fellow polio patient at the table.

"This here is Dillard Runyan. He's been here longer than any of the rest of us. That's Rex who is feeding him."

I said, "Hi," to both of them.

Rex was a big, good-looking guy who gave every indication that he was athletic. His mannerisms and the way he was dressed said so. He was feeding Runyan, a man who made Dennis look like the world's heavyweight boxing champion by comparison. He was skin and bones and hardly anything else. He could swallow, just barely. And, he could just barely get his phlegm up by himself. He could move two fingers on his left hand just a bit, and that was all he had going. Those two fingers were dark brown from nicotine stain. He smoked a lot and often burned his fingers from a lighted cigarette because he couldn't manage to get rid of it before it burned down too short.

With a great deal of effort, he could lean over to his left hand propped up on the arm of his wheelchair and pull deep on the cigarette he was holding in those two fingers. After he sat up straight and blew the smoke out of his nose and mouth, he would wait awhile and then repeat the effort. It darn near wore him out to have a cigarette. When the cigarette burned down short, he had to get rid of it. He did so by leaning down to his left pajama sleeve and grabbing it with his teeth. By pulling back on the sleeve, he could lift his arm free from the arm of the wheelchair and swing it out a bit to the side over the floor.

Then, if he was successful, he would drop the lighted cigarette on the floor for someone else to step on and put out. If his two fingers didn't release, and sometimes they didn't, the cigarette might stick until it began burning his skin. The ensuing stream of basic creative epithets would usually be enough to attract someone's attention to relieve Runyan of his cigarette. Sometimes the cigarette would fall into his lap, and his bathrobe or pajamas would start to smolder. His usual alarm went something like this,

"If it's all the same to the rest of you blockheads, I've got something hot going here in my pants and I don't mean pussy, either. It might be nice if someone put this thing out."

It didn't really bother Runyan too much whatever happened.

He wasn't going anywhere soon, so he just lay back and took things as they came. He had a cigarette after lunch, so I had a chance to see him in action. He had Rex light it for him. It was one of the few pleasures he enjoyed.

He had a rapier tongue most of us tried to avoid. He was sour and ornery and earned the nickname "Onion." But he hadn't given up on life. I really wondered why he hadn't.

Rex and Zim frequently worked his hand, but little resulted. His deep breathing exercises again required a great deal of supervision by Zim or Rex or Satrey from PT. Probably Onion's greatest pleasure in life came when he could sneak up on one of us to grab hold of someone's arm somehow with those two good fingers in his left hand. If he could, he usually pinched the tar out of us.

For him, being able to pinch was a great accomplishment. It usually happened when an evening card game or a checker game was in progress in the ward across from us. That was where most of us spent our free time together. As the interest in the game increased, Onion was overlooked slowly moving his wheelchair across the room.

He made the wheelchair roll forward a bit at a time as he dropped his chin down and then pulled it up with as much of a snap as he could do. He was bobbing his head up and down like mallard ducks bob their heads in courtship, but he was getting his whole body to move forward so the wheelchair would roll.

Ever so slowly, he would make the wheelchair go forward toward his prey, dropping his entire head down, chin first. He had his whole body going. His hand was propped up on the arm of the wheelchair, ready to strike. If he could reach anyone, the pinch was sharp, with his fingernails. If he could draw blood, he was deliriously happy. He got me more than a couple of times. His grin said it all. "Gotcha!"

Zim and Rex were particularly good to Onion. He was so light— under a hundred pounds—they could pick him up with ease. They put him in his bed, in his wheelchair, on the throne in the bathroom, or down on the mats. Wherever he wanted to go. Give him a bath, clean him up. They were gentle with him, almost tender, but he was an obvious prisoner in a pitiful shell called a body, if it even could be called a body.

CHAPTER TWELVE

Swede, Sunporch and Therapy

Putzie, Ed, Mac and I were grouped together in our ward, while in the ward across the hall were Russian, Swede, Onion and Musk-rat—Roy Reineke—who later became Spook. Most of the action was in the ward across the hall or out on the sunporch. Our ward was the quiet one.

I met Trudy that first day when rest time was over after lunch. She was a bouncy little redhead in charge of Occupational Therapy (OT), which lasted for at least a couple of hours every afternoon. We began that day with a volleyball game on the sunporch. Four of us were on each side and Rex on the other to shag the ball. Onion just sat there, but occasionally a ball would bounce off his head and we would cheer. That usually brought a grin to his face.

Playing the game involved stretching the arms, which in turn pulled all kinds of back muscles. It probably helped Swede and Putzie more than the rest of us. But it was good therapy for more than just our bodies. Muskrat, who was laid back anyway, received some verbal jabs to get his long, lanky arms working. He made some good shots when he felt like it.

Sometimes Jean, a slim Red Cross woman, would sit in on our games. It was always a delight to have the younger women like Trudy and Jean involved in our therapy. When Jean shagged a ball, she often bent over farther than she needed to bend, thereby showing us some long, lovely-looking legs with the seams running up the back in her silk stockings. The first time she did that I whispered to Putzie, "Did you see that?"

I didn't even have to look back at him to catch his total disgust at my question.

"What do you think I am, blind? The catheter may be slowing me down some, but it ain't sticking in my eyes to keep me from seeing."

Yes, it was nice having the women in there with us, whatever the reason.

After the volleyball game, we started making Trudy's sewing baskets. Trudy put me on the jigsaw and showed me how to run the blade by pumping the bicycle wheel. When the wheel went around, the jigsaw went up and down. The faster I pumped, the faster the saw went. She shoved the jigsaw over to the bench where the straps were hanging from the overhead poles. There, she harnessed Swede up to the straps so he could hold a clear piece of plastic fairly even to the saw.

"Pump!" she commanded.

I began to pump. The saw began to whiz and Swede moved in from the other side to cut the piece of plastic, the strap from above holding his weak left arm. I found I had to pump harder. It became really difficult to pump as Swede held the plastic to the blade. I couldn't pump very long, and Swede's arms gave out about the same time as my legs did.

"Rest!" called Trudy, and we rested.

I looked at Swede. He was a tall, gaunt man, about my age. Another farmer who had been hit all over by his polio. One leg was weak as were both his arms. That's why he was working on the jigsaw with me. We kept working on the jigsaw for about half an hour, but I was soon tired as was Swede.

After Swede and I cut out a few pieces together, we smoothed them off with the grinder. The grinder worked just like the jigsaw. I pumped it, and Swede held the pieces to the grinder as it went around.

Trudy moved Swede over to another part of the bench where she had some of the plastic pieces in a vise. Swede was supposed to take a rasp in his hands and smooth down the plastic by stroking it. With his arms suspended from the straps, he began to swing back and forth to smooth the plastic.

Somehow, Trudy had Onion rigged up on the other side, trying to get him to do some rasping, but of course he had no muscle power. She might start his arms swinging, with the rasp stuck between the two fingers, but he had no follow through. He had no muscles to keep the swinging up, yet he was involved with the rest of us, and that was the important part of it. Most of the time, Onion just sat in his wheelchair and watched us.

While all this was going on, a woman volunteer was showing me how the big loom worked. I had done some bead work on a small loom when I was a Cub Scout, but this was a big floor loom with two shuttles that had to be worked by my feet. The loom was strung with some lovely pink and blue chenille fabric.

"You could make a beautiful bath mat or perhaps a bedspread," said the woman. I sat down and began to work the shuttle. After I worked it through the strung material, I had to press the lever down with my right leg to shift the set for the next pass of the shuttle. I couldn't quite press the lever down by pushing with my leg, so I had to lift up my right leg with my hands and push it down by hand to move the lever down.

I had to push hard each time, but I began to move the shuttle back and forth, first pushing with my right leg and then with my left. I could just barely push the lever down with my left leg all by itself, but I always had to lift up my right leg by hand and push down down with both hands at the knee to move the shuttle. The pattern of the bath mat began to appear before the afternoon was up, but I became quite tired.

By supper time, I was almost exhausted. I wheeled into my ward and rested on my bed for a while listening to the radio with my headphones on. The next thing I knew, Ed was poking me to tell me it was time to go to supper. I went down in my wheelchair, feeling refreshed from my short snooze.

The evening meal was quite substantial: main dish, potatoes and gravy, vegetable, bread and butter, drink, and dessert. Salad too, if I wanted it. Tonight it was roast chicken. Very good. Like Ed, Swede talked enthusiastically about the food. "Really good chow. Lots better than what I'm used to."

Swede was a bachelor farmer, and he had been doing a lot of running around, burning the candle at both ends, when he came down with polio. So his comment about this being good chow was from the heart. I don't think he was much of a cook, and, besides that, he hadn't spent much time even trying to cook. He told me his story about getting polio while we were cutting out the plastic pieces on the jigsaw.

"I got two bee stings the week before I came down with polio. I know I was run down from all the hell-raising I was doing. Keeping lousy hours. Not eating well, but still, I think those two bee stings out in the milo where I was hoeing the weeds had something to do with my getting polio.

"At first, I thought I just had the flu and thought all I had to do was take it easy. But my head and neck felt like they were in the grip of a giant vise. They hurt and they were so stiff, I finally went to see my doctor.

"Right away, my doctor knew I had polio. He had gone through a mild case of it himself some 20 years before, so he had a good idea of what he was talking about. He told me to go home and stay in bed and take it easy. He told me I probably had polio, but there wasn't much to do for it. Stay quiet and rest was all that could be done.

"So I went home and tried to stay in bed. My sister came over to do a little cooking for me, but I didn't like her coming over much since she might catch it or give it to her kids, or both.

"Then the high fever hit, and I was real groggy. I didn't have no thermometer, but I could tell I was hot. Real hot. Whatever 'it' was that had a hold of me by the back of the neck was working down my spine and into my legs, right into the calves of my legs. They were so tender, I could hardly touch them. I must have gone out of my head some, but I can remember being brought into this hospital by ambulance. They gave me hot packs from the waist down and they sure felt good. They really felt good, but they sure did stink. I think I threw up one time from the stink. The pain shots helped a lot. Made me rest easier.

"Then I began to have trouble breathing. It was awful, trying to take big deep breaths and not having anything happen. Felt like I was suffocating. Couldn't get any air in. The harder I tried to breathe in to take a big breath, the farther away I seemed to be getting from myself.

"I mean, the harder I tried, the more distance there seemed to be between me and my chest, as though I was out behind my chest somewhere. Crazy. I couldn't make contact. Those nurses really worked over me, and somehow, I managed to pull through that one. Never did get into that iron lung, but the nurse told me I came very close. I'm glad I didn't have to use that thing. I had a high fever for about ten days, and some of the time I was very foggy. I'm a lot better now, and sure am glad to be down here with the rest of you guys."

My daily schedule started my second morning right after breakfast. I wheeled into the elevator, went down to the basement, and rolled into PT at 8:30. I was quickly waist deep in an almost hot whirlpool. It lasted for half an hour and I really got loosened up. Felt great. Then back upstairs to my bed for bed exercises. I was to give each exercise 15 minutes. I could see now why we were issued those dark blue gabardine exercise suits. I didn't want to get my pajamas sweaty. Leg lifting: not much accomplished. Like Dennis trying to move his finger, I took the big breath, strained and grunted, and nothing happened. Then I let my breath out, "Ahhhhh." Over on my side, I tried to lift my leg. Right one would go better than the left. Mac was trying to do his stuff, and so was Putzie. Ed was off somewhere, but there were still many grunts coming from our ward. Sit-ups went better. Mac helped me by holding my feet down while I did 25, and that just about ruptured my stomach, it pulled so hard. Then I held his feet down while he did the same.

Zim popped in while we were all working and said, "Keep it up. I don't want any resting until noon, or until I get you out on the mats."

"I can't lift my legs, Zim."

"Don't like 'can't' around here. Let's see . . ."

He watched me straining to lift my legs. I was lying flat on my back, straining as hard as I could.

"Concentrate on what you're doing. You must think about what you're doing. Don't just grunt about it. Here, let's see."

He stuck his palm under my heels and gently began to lift them up. With his help, I could feel something working down there, and then up went my legs. They went up one time.

"Try again."

I tried again. Nothing. He started me out again, and up they went.

"Best you learn how to start. You have some muscles there to do the work. It will come. Switch to another exercise. I'll see you out on the sunporch."

I was puffing when he left, and so I rested a bit.

"Don't rest too long," said Mac. "He'll chew your ass out if he catches you slacking up. He doesn't care a rat's ass about how your feelings may get hurt. He wants you doing exercises and nothing but exercises."

I don't think Mac needed to tell me that, but his urging turned me back to doing my bed exercises. I couldn't do a push-up on the bed, so I got down on the floor and tried.

"Ow!" I cried on the first one. I couldn't do even one, the pain was so intense in the small of my back. I had no strength to keep my back and legs rigid. I just collapsed and gave it up.

"That's something I'll have to keep trying until I can get one in. One will be enough."

My back began to hurt from the strain. And then trying to touch my toes was a further revelation. My fingertips reached only as far as my ankles when the tightness took over. I could feel the pull all the way down my back and into my hamstrings. I had a long way to go. Next, I tried to do a jumping jack and just folded up. Couldn't even come close to getting one started. There was nothing in my coordination that could even begin to get one leap into the air to launch just one jumping jack. I was sweating, and I didn't have any fat on me at 130 pounds. I was down about 18 pounds since I had come down with my polio.

It wasn't long before Zim had us out on the mats on the sunporch. Ed was already there locked in a wrestling match with Muskrat. Both had weak legs and at the moment, Ed was on top. But not for long. Muskrat bit Ed's big toe. Bit it hard. Ed cried out, "Ouch! Ow! That hurts. Muskrat, you're just plain mean."

He turned to rescue his ailing toe, and Muskrat took advantage of his move to turn him even more. Ed quickly found himself lying flat on his back with Muskrat on top, trying to pin him. They both were stretched some in their struggle to win. Mat time was almost always worthwhile time.

Zim turned to me and had me stand up between the parallel bars. He watched me try to walk.

"We must see that you improve your coordination. Remember, I told you, you must think it through. Look in that mirror to see the whole picture, and think that left hip is going to swing forward and not flop out to the side the way it's flopping. Think it through. Russian is right, you do look a little bit like a woman trying to swing her butt out in public. We can't have that in here. Very demoralizing to the troops and besides, it doesn't do you any good. Now, take a step and think that hip forward. Step out and think it. Get your head in that hip as you watch it in the mirror. Remember, you are in control. Who is in control?"

"I am."

"Nope, pull it back and try again. Concentrate! Don't just stand there. Get right into that hip in the mirror. Make it go straight by your own will. It won't come easy. You have to work and work at it, but it will come. Do it again."

That dynamic energy of Zim's was drummed into me, I don't know how many times. Over and over again, I would put my left leg out for a step and be discouraged to see the hip flop out to the side. It played on my mind. Sometimes, when I woke in the middle of the night and couldn't sleep, I would slip into my wheelchair and roll out to the sunporch. There, I would work between the parallel bars for an hour or so until I became too sleepy trying to make the hip go straight.

I'm certain that I put in hundreds of hours between those parallel bars in front of that full-length mirror. That's one of the reasons why I'm walking. But it was a long time before Russian stopped whistling at me. He loved to give me a hard time about my hip flopping out so that from the rear, I looked like a woman swinging her hips, or at least just one hip. Not both. Maybe the reason he gave me such a hard time was that Russian's legs were nothing but toothpicks. Russian spent a lot of time between the parallel bars, too. I just had more to work with than he did. He said many times, "It's all in your head. That's where it is. It's all in your head. You can make your body do anything. It's all there in your head. You can do it if you want to."

I believed him. I believed Russian because I wanted to, and I wanted to walk. I put it in my head to walk again. Russian had nothing but two toothpicks for legs hanging down. That's all he had, and he wanted to walk too.

CHAPTER THIRTEEN

Russian and Recovering

Russian has always been a big man. He must have been a good 225 pounds before he got sick. He worked for a heavy hoist and hauling operation in Omaha and prided himself in being strong. He was that. Ed said that when he wrestled with Russian on the mats it was like trying to get along with a bear, he was so strong. Swede thought Russian had an almost perfect body from the waist up. From the waist down, he had been devastated.

Russian had been married only three days when, on a Sunday, he pitched a double-header softball game. Before the night was over, he couldn't walk. He was wracked with terrific muscle spasms in his legs. He also had a high fever. His doctor diagnosed his case quickly by a spinal tap but made an almost fatal mistake in giving him massive doses of penicillin. He was allergic to the drug and almost died that first night at the Methodist Hospital. He went into a coma from which he emerged four days later when he was moved to the polio isolation ward at County Hospital where Ed and I had been.

Russian's 14-year old brother came down with polio the same day he did, but his paralysis was not nearly as severe. They were both in County Hospital while Ed and I were there, but were probably down at the other end of the isolation ward.

Russian's legs were gone almost immediately, and as far as I could tell, he had gained back very little strength or movement in either. He came to the V.A. Hospital by ambulance about the middle of September just before Ed got there. His wife was extremely anxious for his welfare. The rest of his body was all right. He was cut off at the waist. The thing I noticed the most about Russian was that he was almost always working at trying to get his legs to function—on the mats, between the parallel bars, pulling weights. He was at it all the time.

The exercise I liked best came late in the morning on the sunporch. Zim sat me down on Trudy's bench where my legs hung down free, so they could swing. He said, "I want you to slowly bring your left leg up until it is straight out from you, and then I want you to slowly let it down. Slowly up. Slowly down. No jerking up or flopping down. Slowly up and slowly down will build your muscles in your quadricep. Here, in your thighs are your quadriceps."

He squeezed my left thigh. It was sore.

"You have considerable weakness in your quadriceps in both legs. You've lost your right calf muscle almost completely, and you have a bad slap foot on your left leg. You'll have to develop your hip muscles to get yourself walking again. You can do it. You'll have to learn how to swing your legs out to the side when you walk by using your hip muscles. Right now, we'll strengthen those quadriceps and stretch the hamstrings. Now, begin to bring your left foot up slowly."

I began. I was leaning back a little, resting both hands flat out on the bench behind me, as I began to bring up my left leg. There was no way I could jerk it up. It took all my effort with a deep breath and straining hard, to lift it up straight. As I began to let it down slowly, the pain and strain became overpowering and I let it down with a flop.

"That's just what I don't want you to do, Bob! Let that foot down slowly. Now, do it again."

I know I glared at Zim as he barked at me. Didn't he know my leg was worn out? Did he think I was trying to flop my leg down on purpose? Not much consideration in this guy.

"Okay, I'll try again."

"Forget that 'try' business. Trying is lying. Do it! Do it this time. Like your life depended on it. Concentrate and do it. I don't care if it hurts. It should hurt. You need to get used to working with the pain. Master it. Overcome it with your will. Pain is a natural phenomena. Misery is optional. Get in charge of this program of getting well and walking again. It's your deal. You can do it. It's all in your head. But don't think this is going to take place without pain. Learn to live with it. So what else is new? It's all in your head. Are you in charge?"

Russian glared at Zim when he said that as if he resented Zim's stealing his line, "It's all in your head."

But Russian didn't say a thing.

I took a big breath and brought up my leg. By the time it was up straight, my hamstring was screaming and I was shaking. This time, I did let the leg down slowly. There was sweat on my forehead by the time the leg was down. I finally let the air out, "Ahhhhh." In the pain, I had begun.

Zim didn't ask me to do it again with the left leg. He had me switch to the right leg. It was stronger for this exercise, and I did it up and down three times. It was not easy. My stomach muscle was sore. Screaming. I don't know why I liked this exercise, but I did. Within two weeks, I could do both legs up and down slowly ten times.

When I could do more than ten, Zim had me put on my shoes in place of my slippers.

This additional weight put me back to just two with my left leg and four with my right. Slowly, I worked up to ten again in another couple of weeks. When I could do more than ten, on went an additional five pounds, strapped to my shoes. With this additional weight, I could barely get my left leg up once and no more. My right leg was good for three times. By the time I left the hospital, I was up to 30 pounds on my right shoe and 20 on my left.

It was at our Christmas party the day before I left the hospital that I asked Doc Wilson if he could lift 20 and 30 pounds. He said he could. Russian and I dared him. He saw we were serious in the midst of our joking, so he got up on the bench and strapped on 30 pounds to his right shoe. We made Zim be in charge. I'll never know if Doc was faking or not. He claims he wasn't. But that day, he could not bring up 30 pounds slowly ten times. He gave up at seven. Zim didn't say a word, but we did.

"Doc," Russian said, "we want you in here regularly at 11:30 every morning for these bench exercises with the weights on your shoes to strengthen your legs. They obviously need work. We want you to be healthy as well as set a good example for the rest of us."

This experience with Doc Wilson made me feel as though I had really arrived and was ready for the outside world. But there was a lot of water to go over the dam before I got there, particularly hundreds of hours spent between the parallel bars in front of the full-length mirror trying to walk straight. It must have taken at least a month of hard work before there was a glimmer of progress to my walking.

One thing that did come soon, however, perhaps during the second week at the hospital, was the movement in my right foot. I remember taking the usual big breath, straining down and getting a bit red in the face trying to get my big toe to move up and down. And then it did. It finally did! I yelled and yelled with delight. "Hey look! I can do it! Hey, Zim. Look!"

I'm sure my shouts from the sunporch carried far down the hall into other parts of the hospital. Maybe as many people heard me as heard Putzie when he screamed the time Zim stretched him. It was a breakthrough for me. The first real sign my nerves were coming back and I could get messages through again. I can't tell anyone who hasn't been there what it is like, but I want to.

It was as though I was clean inside. Like the junk in my body, and particularly in my spinal cord, had been wiped away. Of course, never in my life have I ever been able to feel my spinal cord, nor do I ever expect to in the same way that I feel my finger, and yet I knew I had been cleansed all the way inside somehow by a powerful active force. I was beyond my Progressive Polio for good, I hoped. I was okay. I don't know how to put it except to say that I was more alive. I was closer to being whole.

I was joyful I could do it! I was going to move my body again. Too bad I didn't know God then to shout, "Halleluiah!" I was lifted up just the same. I worked between the parallel bars an extra hour or so that day. I could feel some of that stuff Dennis had going for him. I was going to get well. I was going to walk again! Oh, how I needed that sign. It was just what I needed.

An invaluable part of our recovery program at the V.A. Hospital was the fact that we were a group. I was not alone in my agony. Neither was anyone else, including Onion, who made us look like Russian ballet dancers by comparison. We were all there to pick each other up, and that went on constantly, particularly in our horseplay.

When I moved my big toe and let out a shout, the rest of the group was happy for me, and at the same time, each became more determined than ever to work harder. This interaction urged each of us on that much more with a thought something like, "If he can do it, so can I."

I remember the day Russian was working out between the parallel bars and he started shouting because he could lock his right knee. No big deal. It wouldn't lock all the time, but it began to lock some of the time, and for Russian, that was a tremendous step forward.

"Come on, Russian," I said. "You're just working up to taking your first step to swinging your hip like I do. I know you're jealous."

Underneath all the wisecracking was our fervent determination to rise up and overcome the handicaps our polio had inflicted upon us. In the pain, we were there for each other.

CHAPTER FOURTEEN

Hospital Humor

Our recreation and horseplay went on in the other ward. That's where we congregated for poker, checkers, pinochle, or just talking. Swede taught Russian how to play checkers and, for a while, Russian wasn't much trouble for Swede. Slowly things changed. Russian went at learning checkers as he went at recovering from polio, with relentless determination. He even took one of our hospital tables down to the basement some place and had the maintenance people paint a checkboard on it so he wouldn't have to ask the night nurse where she had hidden his checkerboard.

He didn't learn with lightning speed, but what he learned, he did not forget. We would gather in the evening to watch. If anyone else opened his mouth with even the slightest bit of advice, he was out. Banished by the rest of the group. Done. The games became very even. It was during these times of intense concentration that Onion so often did his silent glide across the floor until he "got" one of us with his pinch.

For some reason, we always gave Trudy a hard time about occupational therapy during the afternoons. Whenever there was the slightest chance for ducking out, most of us did. In a minute, we could be almost anywhere else in the hospital in our wheelchairs. They were speedy, and we worked on them to make them even more speedy. We constantly bugged the crew in the maintenance room for oil or graphite for the axles so the wheelchairs would roll with less friction. We could all rock our chairs back on the rear wheels so the front wheels were poised in the air. We had contests on the sunporch to see who could balance his chair the longest. Russian and Muskrat were the best. All of us fell over backwards more than once doing these stunts.

Swede had a clever little trick he enjoyed. Zooming down the hall at high speed, he would race right onto the sunporch and slam into the wrestling mats in his wheelchair. The mats acted as a brake, and Swede would fly right out of his wheelchair onto the mats and land in a heap. The first time Trudy saw him do this, she let out a little scream and thought he was badly hurt.

Swede came up grinning, climbed back up into his wheelchair, raced down the hall some distance, turned around and came flying back to do it again. Trudy was visibly shaken even this second time, but she didn't scream. It was amazing that Swede could generate such speed with his bad left arm, but he had learned how to do it, and it worked. Of course, we wouldn't do things like this when Zim was around. Poor Trudy.

We would have had races, too, in our wheelchairs, but the hospital staff put the damper on that. But we did roam all over the hospital with lightning speed. This drove our night nurse, Old Crotchety, absolutely wild. She had tenure in the hospital, but that's about all she had.

My introduction to her came the first night I was there. About 9:00 o'clock, I was reading in bed when, wham! right in the face, a cold washcloth caught me and slid off to my left ear. Startled, I looked up, and Mac said, "Wash your face with it and shut up if you want to stay out of trouble."

I did and then said, "What do I do with it?"

"Just leave it on your nightstand. She'll get it later."

This was my introduction to Old Crotchety. Each night, she would come to the door of the ward with a basin full of washcloths, slightly damp and slightly cold. Her aim wasn't bad from the door, for in rapid succession, she could hit each one of us with a flying washcloth. When she did miss, we had to pick it up. No one ever complained about her tactics, but it was war forever, undeclared war, against her. Whenever we could, we made life miserable for her. I really believe all of this added to our determination to get well. Her presence stimulated a constant, added adrenalin production.

Nothing else united our group more than our war against Old Crotchety. Together we plotted and hatched ideas against her. We applauded each other's success. United we stood. The very next evening, my second night in the hospital, right after supper, I saw this war take on substance. It became real.

Swede was in happy repose, snoozing on his bed with the earphones on. Ed and Muskrat leaped into action while Old Crotchety was elsewhere. Very carefully, Muskrat reached up and eased the earphones off Swede, whose gentle wheeze never skipped a beat. Then with great effort, they pushed Swede's bed away from the wall and out into the ward toward the door. This was accomplished entirely by arm muscle, as both were pushing from their wheelchairs. Ed had to stop for a moment to wheel over to Onion and move him out of the way, for he had begun to move across the room toward Swede, hoping to pinch an arm that was hanging down. It would have been a sure shot for Onion.

Ed held up a finger to his lips. "Shhh!"

Onion wouldn't always curtail his sharp tongue when requested, but this time he did. Ed rolled him back out of the way. Then, he and Muskrat slowly pushed Swede in his bed to the doorway, and then out into the hall toward the front desk. They made some progress in this direction when Old Crotchety came upon this procession, going down the hallway.

"Where do you think you're going?" she shrieked. Swede was brought directly out of his pleasant snooze to the harsh reality of being in the hallway under Old Crotchety's imposing command.

"Where am I!" he asked sleepily, not seeing Ed and Muskrat behind him pushing the bed down the hall.

"You're out of line, that's what you are. I want to know what's going on here before I call Dr. Wilson and tell him he has three patients who need to be up on Five under lock and key!"

"Oh," said Ed from behind the bed, "we were just going for a stroll. You see, Swede here had the nicest smile on his face as he was snoozing after supper. Muskrat and I began to discuss his dreaming. We began to ponder if external forces such as the gentle rocking of his bed might not alter the content and nature of his dream, don't you know? We were watching the smile on his face to see if this little stroll of ours might indeed change the composition of his dream. You see . . ."

"Get him back in that ward now! This instant! Unless you want me to try some extraterrestrial experiments on both of you."

A crowd had gathered at the end of the hall toward the reception desk. At the entrances to the several wards along the hall, small groups of curious patients had begun to collect.

"Well," said Ed, "we might need some help getting him back in there, and . . ."

"You got him out, you get him back!"

The intensity of Old Crotchety's fury was still rising, and it seemed near a dangerous peak. If she had come by a stroke at that point, I would not have been surprised. Ed and Muskrat sensed they had achieved maximum close hysteria out of her, and dutifully began to return Swede to his place on the ward. They found Onion fuming because no one had thought of wheeling him out into the hall to watch the fun. His outburst truly showed how he viewed himself.

"You simple-minded pimple heads couldn't think of anything except your own fucking fun. I shut up when you told me to be quiet. I gave up getting over to Swede to pinch him. I could have drawn blood out of his arm for sure. It was hanging down just right for a good one. And then you go out and leave me alone in here. You guys are pieces of shit. You aren't even well-formed pieces of shit. You know what you guys are? You are deformed turds. See if I cooperate with you the next time."

The muscles rippled over Muskrat's jaw as he replied with his teeth clenched, "Ah shut up, Onion, before I tie both of your fingers together and shove 'em up your left nostril."

"Now be gentle with Onion, Muskrat," Ed said. "He does deserve better care than what we gave him. You see, Onion, we just didn't have the manpower at the moment. One of the other guys might have helped, don't you know?"

Ed was right. We blew it. Onion seemed to be satisfied, though. He probably got more out of that exchange than if he had been out in the hall watching. Russian challenged the sleepy Swede to checkers, and Onion began watching to see if he had any other chances for a late pinch before the ward shut down for the night.

Old Crotchety went by, and we could hear her muttering, "Why, oh, why did I have to get this bunch? God help me. I need a transfer."

She didn't get a transfer, and two weeks later, it was war again. Because of her tenure, Old Crotchety was given the honor of showing VIPs around now and then. Even though she had the evening shift, she still had her part to play. The hospital liked to show off its evening meal to visitors. That was followed by making rounds of the wards, which was where Old Crotchety liked to shine. Ed understood the fine points of these arrangements and knew how to capitalize on them.

On this particular visitation, Ed might have had prior knowledge that some rather high up V.A. brass was on board and that Old Crotchety was going to strut her stuff that night. Whatever, Ed designed yet another ploy on the snoozing Swede early in the evening. Once again, Swede had fallen asleep with his headphones on.

On the floor of the ward stood an unused I.V. stand equipped with bag, tube, clamp, and nozzle. It had been used to give fluids to a patient recently admitted on the ward. He had suffered a terrible accident when a large tree fell on him. At the moment, he was stable, and so Ed saw far greater possibilities for the use of the patient's idle I.V. unit. It was appropriately available for Ed's plan.

Ed took down the empty bag from the I.V. stand. As soon as we saw him depart with it, we knew a plan was hatching, so we gathered in silence to observe. We were also ready to serve if we were called upon. Zim had already put Onion to bed, so the coast was clear for Ed to operate.

He returned shortly with the bag filled with lukewarm water.

"I don't want cold water because that will be too abrupt a shock to the good Swede. What we're after here is a gradual invasion into the dreams of the snoozing Swede. We could even take bets on the outcome of this venture."

As Ed spoke, he brought the I.V. stand down so he could hook the bag to it with tube and clamp attached. The nozzle was just below.

"I've watched the orderlies and nurses set these contraptions to dripping at just a certain rate, but darned if I've got the combination mastered. Let's see."

Up went the stand. Ed began to play with the clamp and nozzle until he had the drip rate from the bag according to his liking. Then he pulled the stand with its paraphernalia alongside Swede's bed. After some deft maneuvering, Ed arranged the I.V. system to hang directly over the wheezing Swede's head so the nozzle might allow a regular drip of water to fall upon the forehead below. The rate was one drop about every eight seconds. That was according to Ed's calculations.

"I'll take bets that he doesn't wake up inside of a minute. Do I have any takers?"

"I'll bet you two cigarettes," said Russian.

"You're on," said Ed.

We all moved over to Russian's bedside to make it appear as though we were engaged in a game of checkers. From there we watched Swede. The water continued to drip without any apparent change in Swede's dreams. The water began to run down between his eyes and alongside his nose. It looked as if Ed was going to win his bet with Russian, but we never found out.

Old Crotchety arrived at the door with three V.A. VIPs. She was telling them that this was one of the wards for the polio patients and how well we were all doing with some advanced techniques being applied and . . .

"What's happening to that patient over there?" one of the VIPs asked her. As Old Crotchety peered more carefully, I could see the flush on her face rise until it reached her hairline.

She marched up to Swede's bed and, in a booming voice which jolted Swede back to reality yet another time, she almost bellowed, "This looks like someone's idea of a joke. Well, I can tell you it's not a joke to misuse government property, and someone will pay for this. I'll see to it, you can be sure."

She grabbed the I.V. stand and yanked it across the floor towards the door. This abrupt action somehow wrenched the clamp loose and the bag immediately emptied all over the floor, leaving a puddle of water. She was so speechless with rage, she could do nothing but usher the VIPs on to another ward.

We muffled our laughter in glee. My sides hurt keeping my laughs in. Swede was in a daze.

"Where did I get all of this water?" he asked, still not realizing what had happened.

"Come over here and play me a game of checkers," said Russian. "I'll tell you all about it. You were safe from Onion tonight, but not from Ed."

About a month later, Russian had his turn. He had a little plastic beetle his wife had brought him for some reason. It didn't take long for him to find a good use for it. The chance came at the end of our evening snack when Old Crotchety brought us milk and cookies. She really hated bringing us the snack; she certainly didn't think we deserved it or needed it.

Russian put the beetle in the bottom of his milk glass and waited. Old Crotchety came in and started the usual banter, "Well, did any of you nice veterans gain any needed weight from your precious snack?"

"Nope. I might have lost a little from it, though."

"Now, Russian, what makes you say such an encouraging thing like that?"

"I found a beetle in the bottom of my milk glass. Couldn't finish the rest after that. Who knows what else I might find in this milk."

"Let me see what you're talking about."

Old Crotchety took Russian's glass. Suspicion was all over her face, but she could clearly see the beetle sloshing around in the bottom in some milk. Russian had left the right amount of milk in the bottom to help make the beetle look real yet visible. She easily took the bait.

"You know, we've been having some trouble with this milk

company lately. Give me that thing. I'm going to report it to our supervisor. We can't have this sort of thing going on. It isn't healthy for you men."

She took the glass and marched away in pomp and circumstance to do in the poor milk company. We all enjoyed a bit of fulfillment in the silence that followed, particularly Russian. He said, "I think I'll go for a roll in my wheelchair."

Off he went, humming a little tune. Old Crotchety never got back to Russian to give him the satisfaction of this prank, but Russian came back more quickly that evening than expected.

A rescue team brought him back. He was lying on a cart and Muskrat came in on another cart soon afterwards. They had had a bad collision at an intersection of two hallways up towards One North where they both had been speeding along. Russian had bent several fingers as he went sprawling, and Muskrat had bruised his face when he fell into one of the big wheels. It must have been a spectacular crash. Both wheelchairs were almost beyond repair. Old Crotchety didn't breathe a word.

Next day, Doc Wilson said plenty.

"I'm taking your flashy fold-up wheelchairs away from all of you. You guys are too dangerous. Two of you got hurt last night. Next time, it could be one of the other patients. You all are getting the old wooden wheelchairs with the big front wheels and the little back ones that swivel. You can get around in them, but not fast. I simply can't take the risk of an even worse accident happening than the one you two guys had last night.

"It has also been reported to me that there have been several 'near misses' lately at other intersections, one involving a medical cart with test tubes and flasks. The operator of that cart had to swerve quickly to avoid collision, causing several of the test tubes to spill."

We were grounded.

CHAPTER FIFTEEN

Holy Water and Walking

Gone were our lightweight, folding, speedy wheelchairs except for one occasion. When we all went swimming on Thursday afternoons at the Y.M.C.A. pool in downtown Lincoln, we had to take the speedy wheelchairs. Everyone went swimming except Putzie, who still had his catheter.

Leaving the V.A. to go swimming was like going into a different world. We went in a big van and had a good look at the outside world. We were out of the hospital. That was good for all of us who unknowingly had become terribly institutionalized and dependent upon the system. The physical departure from the hospital allowed us a chance to change our behavior and attitudes. It was a nurturing change for us. The actual experience of getting into that pool provided even more opportunity for change.

I'll never forget the first time I slipped into that pool and found myself waist-deep in water where I could actually walk and move up and down on my toes. I was elated. As I see that scene now so vividly, it was as though I was hearing a symphony orchestra coming up full—strings and horns going all out. Joyful music surely was filling that whole place. I was overcome by a profound feeling of freedom. I looked down at my poor legs in the water almost in disbelief.

A new dimension was written into my life. My walking in the water was a miracle! This experience was transforming beyond all doubt. The ugliness of my polio was gone. Again, I felt clean and new. The grip polio had on me was gone for a while at least, and I was free! Free! First my big toe, and now both legs were working.

I just knew I was setting out on a high adventure. It was like being on a frontier. You didn't know what to expect over the next hill, but you knew something new and interesting and rewarding was just ahead. And you pressed on to find out.

Perhaps it was my own euphoria that painted the scene before me, but I believe that there was a smile of exhilaration on all the faces in the water. Even Onion, bobbing around in a life jacket, had a new face. He wasn't smiling exactly, but he seemed peaceful. Zim was working with him in the water. Zim had always been insistent that in the water, he could get some feeble but noticeable side kick movement out of Onion's left leg. I never saw it, but I know that simply being in the water was a comforting change for his emaciated body of just skin and bones. He didn't have any padding left to his body, no fat or muscle to cushion him. So now, in the water, he too was free, free from the pressure on his skin and bones while sitting in his wheelchair. He was floating with ease, soaking it all up. It was a new birth for him, too.

I don't know how long our swimming periods lasted. They were never long enough. Almost every time we went, though, we didn't come back until we had almost drowned each other in water polo. Onion was the only exception; we did not drown him, although at times he accidently bobbed into our line of combat. Then we would call "time" and push him out of the way. We did this for his own safety and also to avoid his razor sharp tongue. He had the capacity for making any of us look like idiots in short order. We had heard him cut his wife Charlotte down with equal sharpness. So as best we could, we kept from splashing him. Just the same, we did get caught up in the game almost to a frenzy.

The buoyancy of our bodies in the water allowed all of us to walk to some degree except Russian. For me it was somewhat like finding I had new parts to my body, and I was experimenting with them, trying to get them to work. Being in the water was wonderful.

I could feel my weak muscles moving, coming to life. Standing chest-deep, I could rise up and down on tiptoe with my right foot, while I could do the same at just waist-deep with my left. I marked the spots in the pool where I could accomplish these feats and then next time I came, I would try to move into more shallow water to see if I could move up and down on my tiptoes there. If I could, that meant my legs were getting stronger. The progress was slow but sure, and that was exciting. Living was beginning to have more value.

While Zim worked with Onion, Rex became involved in our therapy, which consisted mainly of water polo. Rex was a beautiful swimmer and diver, an all-around fine athlete. He also did some high school football and basketball refereeing. He was good natured and we all liked him.

Russian, Ed, and I as a team stood Rex, Swede, and Muskrat in water polo across the shallow end of the pool. We used a plastic ball about the size of a volleyball. Our water polo was something apart and different from the rest of the treatment and therapy we received. In the mad confusion of trying to make a goal, weak muscles were forgotten. When Rex had the ball, Russian and I would converge on him to all but drown him.

Russian was a big man, and even though his legs were dead weight, he was still a hard man to get away from. He was incredibly strong. His one disadvantage was that when he got the ball, he could swim with only one arm. He quickly developed a technique of taking a big breath and then plunging ahead. Since he could barely keep his head above water swimming with one arm, this worked better. He was hard to stop this way until Muskrat figured out a simple solution. Even though his legs were quite weak, Muskrat could still stand in the water waist-deep rather well. So he stood in Russian's way and as Russian came up for air, Muskrat simply reached out a hand and held Russian's head down in the water. Russian stayed down until he gave up the ball. Much pool water went into Russian before he gave up the ball. Somehow, this disadvantage didn't seem fair to Russian. We found a float and tied it around his middle so the dead part of his body didn't drag him down anymore. Now, Russian could plow through the water like a powerful scow, and that's what he did.

The first time the Good Ship Russian rammed the Muskrat, it was a different story. Muskrat had to get his legs moving to keep up with the scow. In the frenzy of the game, Muskrat would forget how weak his legs were. He moved. He moved quickly. There would be a terrible spash, and sometimes Muskrat would come up with the ball. Then, did he ever move toward Ed, trying to score a goal! He simply forgot how weak his legs were and how far they could be stretched.

The tall, lanky Swede was goalie for Muskrat and Rex. His arms were weak. He had a hard time raising them up and back. But in the midst of a drive by Russian or me, Swede would take a step or two out to meet the attack on very shaky legs. The fight would en-sue and, quite often, Swede would have to reach way up and back to block a shot. What he did as goalie was more than he could do in the sunporch on the mats and at the weights.

At the other end of the pool, the same was true for Ed, who was our goalie. His trouble was trying to get his trunk up straight. He had overall weakness in his lower back. In addition, his polio had tightened his hamstrings and lower back so badly, he couldn't stand up straight. He couldn't, that is, until he found himself in a do-or-die save situation against Muskrat or Rex. Then Ed could more than straighten up high; he could reach way up to block the shot. He wouldn't even have time to be surprised at what he had just done because the splash after the blocked goal would find him in a death fight for the ball at the goal. I really don't know why one or two of us didn't drown in the scrambling we went through to score a goal. The game was all-out aggression, and we simply threw ourselves into it. An extravaganza of abandonment. When our time was up, we were exhausted and happy. I know we all stretched arms and legs more in the battle than we could possibly do in our exercises back at the hospital.

Most of us tried to do our exercises faithfully at the hospital, but they were so boring. It was so hard, day after day, to keep giving it all we possibly could. In the pool, in the midst of a fight for the ball, we were all doing things with our arms and legs which were unreachable back at the hospital. What we were doing was fun, different, and competitive. What a contrast that was to being told what to do and when to do it all day long in the hospital. We were alive in the pool, and we knew it. Our time at the pool was special time, valuable time, very important time. Not the kind of time measured by a watch. Life time. We were growing in this highlight of our week.

When we came back, we always made a beeline for the PX down the basement. As a matter of fact, we usually managed an afternoon coffee break to the PX every day, but the trip to the PX after swimming on Thursdays was different. Our high spirits were still with us. We would enter the PX in a line in our flashing wheelchairs, each man leaning on the handles of the chair in front, Onion in the lead, and I usually pushing from the back. We were in our dark blue gabardine exercise suits that set us apart from the rest of the patients in their pajamas and bathrobes.

We simply took over the PX when we came in. We were the playboys of the hospital at least until we lost our sleek wheelchairs. In the PX, we were boisterous and made passes at the young girl behind the counter. We just gave everyone a hard time in there. It was great being totally alive for a while.

There came a time when Zim decided to take my wheelchair away. This was still back before Doc took away our flashy chairs. Right after breakfast, as I prepared to head down to PT for my morning whirlpool, Zim came into the ward. "Bob, I want you to walk down to PT this morning."

I was surprised, and then I wasn't. Zim was so straight and blunt and tough. There was no use arguing. I walked to PT that morning. I spent most of the morning getting there.

I started out from my ward and got into the hall successfully, heading for the elevators back toward the reception desk. In the ward, I was able to hold onto things to keep my balance, but once out in the hall, it was a different story. Three steps and I fell down when my right knee wouldn't stay locked.

I wasn't hurt. I had rolled a bit with the fall the way Dennis had. Getting up was another matter. I couldn't get up. Zim and a couple of friends watched from the doorway of the sunporch. No one moved to help me up. I scrambled around on the floor, but there was no way I could get up. My legs couldn't do it. There was nothing in the hallway to hang onto so I could pull myself up. The group at the doorway watched in silence.

I felt resentment. I was mad and proceeded to garnish my anger with a large dollop of self-pity.

"They don't care at all," I thought to myself.

I tried again to get up but slipped back down. More anger. A thought came to me. I scooted on my butt over to the wall. Sitting up straight with my legs straight out in front of me with my back to the wall, I placed the palms of my hands flat against the wall on each side of me where the wall meets the floor.

I pushed up on my body by pushing down on my hands. I tried to push back with my feet, but there wasn't much push there. Most of the work was coming from my arms as my body began to rise. Keeping one hand flat on the wall, I raised the other hand up higher, and again with the palm flat on the wall, I pushed down on that hand to raise up my body some more. It was like backward swimming. I switched to using my bare feet to keep my legs straight and locked in so I wouldn't slip back. I wasn't always successful in keeping my legs straight, but most of the time I was.

Slowly, I literally inched up the wall, pushing up on my palms, pushing back with my feet and keeping my legs straight to keep my trunk rigid against the wall and locked. No sign of encouragement from the group at the doorway as I got up at last. I glared at them and started off down the hall. After another three or four steps, down I went again. I hated Zim. I was more uptight this time, anticipating the fall, and so I banged my right elbow as I went down.

I sat up and rubbed it and then scooted over to the wall again. I repeated the rising procedure, only this time, about halfway up, I slid back down and had to start all over again. Still the group watched, and then Zim broke it up and told the rest of the guys to get going about their morning schedule as he walked toward the sunporch to work with Onion.

I fell down 36 times getting to PT that morning. By the time I arrived, I had learned how to fall in a relaxed manner and roll with the flow of the fall. I had developed the scooting up the wall almost to perfection and was learning how to keep my right knee locked. Trying a number of different techniques, none of which worked, I marveled at myself for the concentration I was attaining in dealing with my knee problem.

By the time I reached the PT room, I was over my anger; I just couldn't afford it. I had replaced it with learning how to fall. I remembered how Dennis had fallen into his wheelchair back in Omaha. Some people did it naturally and others came by it harder, but I had the feeling of accomplishment.

I knew how to fall, and I had gotten there. No one else could have given that to me. I had done it for myself. Somewhere in this experience there had been some tough love, but I didn't like it. Zim didn't care about that part. All he said to me later on during the day was, "You made it."

And so I had.

Ed came up to me that evening and said, "I watched you falling down trying to make your way to PT this morning. That was hard work, but that's what it takes. I've been working on going upstairs using my Canadian sticks. You know, I have to swing my leg out to the side to get it to move forward or up. When I come to a step, that's what I do. I swing my right leg up on the step. Then comes the hard part. I take off the sticks and hold them in my left hand which I also use to hang onto the railing. This frees my right hand which I use to push down hard on my right knee. That straightens my right, locks the knee, and moves me up on that leg. Now, I am free to swing my left leg up to the same step and then I repeat the action. It's slow, but it works, particularly if a person wants to go up some stairs, don't you know?

"I've fallen down a couple of times doing this, but so far I haven't been hurt. Always manage to grab the railing with my right hand before I fall too far. Gotta watch how you do it, else a person could really get hurt."

"Yah," I said, "It takes a lot of hard work."

What I didn't say was that I appreciated his coming up to me and sharing. I felt that he was supporting me, and that meant a great deal to me. I was thinking about walking down to PT the next day, and it was good to know someone felt kindly toward me. The support felt good.

CHAPTER SIXTEEN

Spook and Long Legs

Both Ed and Russian smoked, and it was along about when I first walked to the PT room that they began to rag each other about smoking. They each proposed that they both stop. Hearing them tell each other how they were going to be free from smoking was beautiful. Two con artists were at work. The icing on the cake of their agreement was this: If either caught the other smoking a cigarette, the offender would have to pay one dollar. They both quickly became expert liars and cheats. It soon appeared that both were more interested in tricking the other than they were in stopping. Their pact of not smoking proved to be great entertainment to the rest of us.

Once, Ed came rolling into the ward and challenged Russian that he had been smoking.

"No," said Russian.

"My nose tells me there was a cigarette in here only moments ago, but darned if I can see one."

A few moments later, the wastepaper basket next to Russian's bed began to smudge, but Ed had his back to it at first so he didn't see it. Russian was so deeply engrossed in the latest edition of "The Sporting News" that it was hard to believe that he might have anything to do with yonder smoking basket. Stranger still how Russian further managed to spill an entire glass of water from his checkerboard hospital table into the wastebasket. That was when Old Crotchety appeared in the doorway to the ward, apparently feeble and weak-hearted from coughing,

"My God! What are you smoking in here, or is it time to call the Fire Department?"

"Forget the Fire Department," Ed said. "I think I just lost a buck. I sure can't keep up with Russian, neither on the mats or on the ward. He's too slick for me."

Russian managed a weak grin, but I could see a wisp of smoke curling out of his nose. Ed never saw it for the wastebasket held his curious thoughts and attention. It had really been smoking. So had Russian.

Another place of entertainment for us turned out to be PT room in the morning after breakfast. There we were being stretched, rubbed, and scrubbed when we weren't in the whirlpool. Even though he couldn't go to the swimming pool with us, Putzie was able to sit in a whirlpool with his catheter hung over the side. How he loved to sit there and read his newspaper. Next to beer, this was it for Putzie.

Muskrat, a most perceptive person, sensed this great feeling of well-being on the part of Putzie. He decided to get some mileage out of the situation. He calculated it was time for some "hot news" in the hospital. He lit Putzie's paper with a match one morning and rolled back in his wheelchair a few feet to watch the result. He was not disappointed.

The flame shot up on the newsprint and Putzie gave a jerk trying to get rid of the flaming paper. His hands were slightly damp, so they stuck to the paper. His singed hands and eyebrows were Muskrat's bonuses for the prank. His humor seemed satisfied by Putzie's mishap, and for a while, Putzie was unsure who had done the deed. Muskrat smirked. He loved it. No matter that it might have been a serious accident. We all began to keep a more careful eye on Muskrat.

Muskrat was also expert at flicking a bath towel so the sting was maximum on arm or leg. "Snap," the sound and "zing," the sting when he got you. Again his smirk showed his pleasure. We all re-taliated to his attacks, but he was the champ. He had a flair and a grace to his precision shots. We all had welts to show his accuracy.

The PT room was a lively place for so early in the morning. But now we had to keep an eye on Muskrat because he could have your pants tied in hard knots to someone else's in scarcely any time at all. Muskrat was always hovering and lurking, ready to strike, which he often did. His behavior made us a bit uneasy.

Swede suffered more than one "hot foot" from him at various times. For some reason, Russian never participated in this early morning PT time, and I wondered if it might not be that some hard feelings existed between Russian and Zim. I think if Russian had been part of the action around the whirlpools, Muskrat might not have been so successful at bullying. To him, it seemed to be only good fun. Muskrat was a good, hard, tough person.

I think his early morning aggressiveness was the outlet for his polio anger and fear. Early in his recovery with us, he had often withdrawn noticeably by simply pulling up the sheets over his head and staying in bed for lengthy periods. A great deal of anger and fear was connected with polio; when Muskrat came out from under his sheets, he was getting some of these feelings off his chest—but at our expense.

Toward the end of October, I found myself spending more and more time between the parallel bars. When I couldn't sleep at night or when I would wake up in the middle of the night, I would just ease myself into my wheelchair and slip out to the sunporch. The lights on there didn't bother anyone, and I spent hours taking the steps.

Out would go my left foot and the strain of concentration would come as I tried ever so hard to keep that hip from flopping out. At the same time, I had to shift concentration on the same leg to keep the left foot from slapping down as I completed the single step. I think my concentration was sharper now because I was paying intense attention to my body movements during morning walks to PT.

This was exhausting work, and I usually didn't stay between the parallel bars too long. These nighttime exercises usually put me to sleep rather quickly when I crawled back into bed. An hour was about all I could do at a time. The left hip was getting there. Russian wasn't whistling at me so much during my daytime workouts.

We also found that Zim was urging us to wrestle on the mats more and more. This was somewhat like swimming in that the struggle to pin or not be pinned found all of us straining and stretching more than we would do in regular exercises.

We all wrestled each other, but the best match-ups were Swede and Muskrat, and Russian and Ed. Russian would play with Ed and force him to strain his back and leg muscles. Swede and Muskrat were almost dead even except for biting. Muskrat would lie back and give the appearance of being done in except he had the ability to slither out of Swede's grasp. Swede's left arm and hand were weak. But the second time Muskrat bit Swede—this time not on the big toe, but on the right arm—Russian and I decided Muskrat needed to be skinned, at least a little.

Even though he was in considerable pain most of the time and suffered from weak legs, Muskrat was still dishing out misfortune to us at an unacceptable level. The fire of Putzie's newspaper, the knotted pants almost all of us had endured, added up to more than enough. Swede had had one pair of shoes burned slightly by a hot foot, and I had some slippers that were black in the middle from the same trick by Muskrat. Anyway, Russian and I were prepared to slow him down.

We found the perfect chance for fixing Muskrat when Long Legs Jean came around from the Red Cross to tell us we were going to have a hospital Halloween party in the auditorium and that a "Spook" was going to be elected from amongst the patients and "crowned" at the party.

"Muskrat will make a perfect spook," I said to Russian. "Let's get going. We'll go around to the other wards and talk them into voting for Muskrat and then spring it on him right there at the party. That should hold him for a while. He may even have to go around to the other wards to put in guest appearances. Should keep him busy and us out of trouble."

"I hope he flies right out here on his broom," said Russian.

So we set out in our wheelchairs and began campaigning for Muskrat. It wasn't so hard to get the patients in the other wards to go along with Muskrat as Spook. Within two days, Russian and I had most of the hospital lined up. We told the other patients that we had a guy in our group who definitely needed to be elected "Spook," and we needed their help.

It wasn't long before Long Legs got wind of our scheme and became upset with us because she had expected nominations and campaigning all to take place at the party.

We explained to Long Legs what we were up to and she became amused, but not totally happy. Still, we had gone so far she couldn't get it turned around, so she accepted what we had done. We had the ballots already signed by Halloween, and then somehow Muskrat found out the day of the party what we had been up to. He said flat out, "I won't do it."

"Muskrat, you would make a wonderful spook," I said.

"Won't do it."

"Muskrat, you've earned it," said Russian.

"Won't change my mind."

"Look, Muskrat, it's all set; the ballots are in," I said, "it's all planned to crown you 'Spook' of the hospital. I've written a first class epic poem about you. You deserve it and it fits you. You can't back out. Here, take a listen," I said. "I'll read a bit of it to you."

Here's to our "Spook"
on Halloween,
who's cross and sly
and always mean.

At night along our
dingy halls,
his witchcraft art
and spooky calls,

he practices with
wild delight,
brews his visions with
all his might.

"And on it goes. There's two pages of it. It's perfect to crown you 'Spook.' You'll be famous. Everyone will look up to you and say, 'There goes the Spook.' Maybe Old Crotchety will even bring you your evening washcloth. There's lots in it for you, Muskrat. What do you say?"

"I don't care anything about all that shit. I don't want to be known as 'The Spook.' Get someone else."

I could tell Muskrat was beginning to feel very uneasy, and he seemed to be set on not being the Spook.

"Look," said Russian, "suppose we dress you up as the Spook. Put a sheet over you and cut eye holes and a mouth hole. Disguise you so no one will know who you are. Would you be willing to do it that way?"

By this time, the rest of the guys were huddled around us out on the sunporch. They all knew what was going on, and pretty much the whole group said, "Come on, Muskrat."

He squirmed and then said, "Okay, I'll do it, but you've got to cover me up with a sheet like you said, Russian."

Trudy heard this conversation, as it had gone on during after-noon occupational therapy, and she jumped right in.

"I'll have housekeeping find an old sheet, and we can cut out the holes for the eyes and mouth and color in some lips and eye-brows. Maybe we could even get a mop for some hair. I'll get on it right away."

Just then Long Legs came in and Trudy asked her, "Is there going to be a queen crowned, too?"

"Hadn't thought of that," said Long Legs.

"I'll bet we could get one elected from amongst the nurses and nurses' aides."

"Great!" said Long Legs. "The guys will have more fun electing a queen at the party anyway. I'll get busy and round up some of the nurses to stay for the party so we can be sure to have someone to elect."

We didn't have much time left as the party was slated for seven o'clock. Long Legs and Trudy went into high gear, and the results were great. Spook got his wish, but I think he also got the message. Maybe he thought he never belonged before, but I think the election of Spook won him over. After the party he really settled down and became easier to get along with.

We elected a queen; and she and Muskrat, now redubbed "Spook," reigned at a great party. Long Legs did a fantastic job emceeing the party and took every occasion to show the whole hospital that she had some pretty good looking legs.

It was a great party. And as I said, after the party, Spook seemed to be a changed person. He didn't give us any more grief and actually became much friendlier. It worked out much better than we had planned. There was a good feeling all the way around.

Another nice result of the Halloween party was the more visible presence of Long Legs. She almost became part of our group, through planning many more activities for us. Three of us—Putzie, Swede, and I—weren't married but she didn't show any partiality to any of us. She was good at planning activities to get us out of the hospital.

We even asked her to go swimming with us, but she passed on that one when she heard we went skinny dipping. But she arranged for us to visit a bomber at the Lincoln Air Base and used an extra long ramp so the wheelchair patients could get in. I went on crutches and blistered my hands a little. It was great to get out. I remember the pilot of the bomber didn't miss Long Legs' long legs with the seams up the back.

Long Legs also found us some tickets to the Oklahoma-Nebraska football game. The guys in the wheelchairs sat on the field at the corner of the end zone, but Rex and I had seats up in the stadium. Again, I went on crutches, but this time, my hands were hardened and didn't blister.

I soon found that I was frightened in the big crowd. I wasn't around all the familiar people and places of the hospital, and I was unbelievably scared. I was surprised at myself because I had been an adventuresome person. Going into the bathroom with everyone else so close and pushing was pure agony. After my initial fright, I began to see just how institutionalized I had become. It took me a while to figure it out, and then I could hardly believe what was going on inside me. The pain and fear I was going through was good for me, but I didn't like it. Just as Russian said, "It's all in your head."

After the game, Long Legs found me and asked me if I wanted to come over to her apartment for a drink before heading back to the hospital. I couldn't say "yes" fast enough.

"Rex," I said, "Long Legs is going to get me a ride back so I'll be going with her."

"Fine," was his reply.

I wondered how I deserved getting this break. If this was part of the therapy, I'd take it any time. We chatted in her car about how things were going at the hospital. She lived on the second floor, so it wasn't too hard a climb for me on the crutches. Once in her apartment, I could move around freely, so I put the crutches aside. I didn't know how long it had been since I had had a drink, but it was over three months. The Scotch and water tasted good to me, and so did the nice kiss that went with it. It was more like a peck, but it was still a kiss, and a few bells and whistles went off inside me. What a day for swings in emotion.

"Here's to your progress and your spunk," Long Legs said as she raised her glass to me. I felt great, and part of that great feeling was the surge of masculinity I felt. It was hard for me to believe I was where I was. My heart was pounding a bit, and I knew it. I had another drink, but there wasn't another kiss to go with it.

"You're a nice guy, and I hope with all my heart that you keep right on recovering the way you are. Let's keep it as friends. Okay?"

What else could I say but, "Fine." Of course I wanted to say more. She was a very warm person and I wanted to say any number of things to her. But I was aware of some real frustration on my part. Her close presence was almost overpowering me with desire.

Long Legs sensed that in me and decided it was time to get me back to the hospital. We had a quick bite at her place, so I gladly missed eating dinner at the hospital. What kind of steps had I taken today other than the ones Zim wanted me to take? The outside world was getting closer. I was very glad to be alive.

Russian noticed that I came back late. Maybe he could smell the liquor on my breath; he was more than a bit suspicious. "Get a little special treatment after the game?"

I wondered to myself if he had seen me with Long Legs, so I decided to smoke him out. "Boy, did I ever! I met this gorgeous creature just as I was coming out of the stadium. She didn't see Rex. She just saw me and took pity on me on my crutches. And Russian, she took care of me. She was so beautiful, and she had this gorgeous house and she isn't married, and . . ."

"Shut up, Hall."

It was like back in the Army barracks and all the BS about all those women who were gorgeous and desirable who just happened to shower some guy with all their charms. Russian had heard it all before. But he didn't find out where I had been, and I guess he figured he wasn't going to find out. But then, maybe he already had it figured out.

CHAPTER SEVENTEEN

A Pistol, Frey and Russian's Review

Our entire group of polio patients was young compared to the average age of patients in the hospital. A good number of World War I patients were all around us, so we were the "youngsters" in the hospital. Zim wasn't much older than we were, and Trudy and Long Legs were about the same age as Zim. So there was a real contrast between what went on around us and the rest of the hospital.

In the first ward down the hall from us was an old man named Cooney, who had arthritis in his hands about as bad as I could imagine. All of his fingers were absolutely rigid, but more than that, they were grotesque. Several of the end joints in his fingers bent backwards in their rigid position. He couldn't do anything like feed himself or take care of his bodily functions.

About the only thing Cooney could do was get around in his wheelchair, which he did by digging his heels into the floor and pulling himself forward. He had one of the old-fashioned wheel-chairs like the ones we were blessed with after Spook and Russian had their accident. I remember watching Cooney scratch himself one time with one of those rigid crooked fingers, and I had to turn away, it bothered me so.

I had hope. I wondered how much Cooney had, and yet I never heard him complain once, even though I knew he had a great deal of pain. He had to have pain in his hands the way they were so tightened by the rigidity and tension in the end joints. I could see the skin was extra smooth over the ends of his fingers. He was probably going to spend the rest of his life right there. We were all working on getting out of there, and we expected to. We didn't have to look around too far to realize just how lucky most of us were. I think Cooney told us he had already been there over six years.

As far as facilities and care were concerned at the hospital, we really had a blessing we did not even realize. The therapy was almost priceless, it was so advanced. In almost any other hospital, almost all of us would have been left to stay put in our beds with but the mildest of exercises. Our sunporch itself was a show place for the kind of care we needed. The V.A. was not lacking for funds in any way, and we received the best care there was.

Between Halloween and Thanksgiving, we all made considerable progress except for Onion. He never got beyond the use of just two fingers. One Saturday afternoon when he and Putzie were left behind while the rest of us went to a football game, Onion began to be more than mildly interested in Putzie's .32 caliber pistol he had at home. Putzie had talked several times about the target shooting he had done with it. His skill at hitting the target had come along to the point where he was almost a sharpshooter.

Putzie wasn't one to brag. This was just information he revealed over the weeks we were all together. We naturally talked about hunting, guns, fishing, and so on. So we all knew Putzie had a .32 at home. This particular Saturday afternoon, Onion grew most interested in that gun.

"Did you ever think of bringing your gun down here to the hospital?" Onion asked.

"What would I want to do that for?" said Putzie, a bit surprised.

"Oh, I'd like to see it. Maybe we could go outside somewhere and shoot it for practice. Never did handle a hand gun myself while I was in the Army. I wonder if I could shoot it with my finger. Maybe I could if someone stuck it in my lap so I could get my finger on the trigger."

"Seems to me you might end up shooting yourself that way," said Putzie. "I sure wouldn't stick it in your lap so you might get your finger on the trigger."

"That might not be the worst thing that could happen," Onion speculated.

Putzie felt very uncomfortable, but he also had a great deal of compassion for Onion.

"Man, you can try to kill yourself if you want to, but I want no part of it. I know you've got it bad, but my .32 isn't coming to this hospital. Ever!"

Maybe that's when Onion hit bottom. It probably was necessary for him to think about something like ending his life before he could start back up. He was in terrible shape and had little hope, but I can honestly say that I never got the message from him that he had quit. He was always a very important member of the group. We accepted him for the way he was, and we all helped him when we could. But I don't think he ever received any pity from us. We were all equal in the group, Onion included. Putzie told me that when he finally got out of the hospital and went home, "I found that .32 pistol and had such a bad feeling about it, I got rid of it. It just gave me the shivers when I picked it up and got to thinking about that conversation with Onion."

Shortly after the Halloween party, we received a new patient on our ward. His name was Frey. He was an older man who had been afflicted by a stroke. He could walk some, but he used a cane and he dragged his left leg badly. He was terribly frustrated because all he could say was, "One time."

Doc Wilson told us Frey had been working in the oil fields at Bakersfield, California, when he had the stroke. That was why he was pointing to the west when he said, "One time." His home was at Sidney, Nebraska, also to the west of us. Doc told us that Frey was a deeply religious man. He was placed in our ward so he could receive therapy for his dead left arm and badly retarded left leg.

He valiantly tried to join in with the group, and his eye contact with us was most unusual. Since he couldn't talk, his eyes carried his conversation for him, and most of us got his messages to some extent by watching his eyes. They were most expressive, opening wide, narrowing to slits, crying, laughing, proud and lonely.

Zim and Rex worked with Frey and he quickly became another member of the early morning group at the PT room around the whirlpool. Frey got his turn, too. His broad smile told us he liked the sensation of the water in the whirlpool. Zim did not allow him to have a wheelchair. Frey had to walk to and from PT as I was doing. He did, slowly, and with considerable patience. I had almost forgotten about patience until I found myself watching him slowly make his way down the hall. Step and drag the left leg. Step and drag again.

He must have made some improvement while he was with us, but I never saw it. He worked hard. Trudy worked his dead hand. She rubbed it, flopped it, tried to get him to squeeze a rubber ball. All to no avail. He went regularly to some place in the hospital for speech therapy, but he made no progress there either. "One time" was all he could say. I think the best thing that happened to Frey at the hospital was being included in our group.

We kidded him and waited for him sometimes when he was so

slow and even hollered at him. So he knew he belonged. That was the most we could do for him. When he cried, which was often, we didn't belittle him for it.

Thanksgiving came, and I was allowed a pass to go out with Mother and Long Legs for the day. Since I was barely walking, I wore slippers so I wouldn't have too much weight on my feet. On my left leg, I wore a garter, but not the kind Russian would whistle at. The garter was just below my knee and attached to it was a spring which came down to the slipper. The spring let my foot down easy so it wouldn't slap so badly. It was awkward, but it worked.

My left hip was still flopping out some, but it certainly was better. I tried going without crutches. Mother drove down from Omaha and we went out for dinner and drove around for a while. Naturally, I overdid, and when I came back early in the evening, I was tired. There was some kind of movie showing in the auditorium, so both wards were empty except for Frey in our ward. He was lying on his bed with the earphones on listening to the radio. I called, "Hi," to Frey as I came to the door and he replied, "Hi," to me. He was looking right at me, but I could tell he was also half listening to the music in the earphones. Just the same, I realized he had said "Hi" to me instead of "One time."

"How are you?" I called from the doorway.

"Fine," he said.

"Where's everybody else?"

"They've all gone away some place."

He was speaking clearly and distinctly. No slurs. No evidence of a stroke in his speech.

"Wait a minute, Frey, I'll be right back," I called from the doorway. There was no one around for me to tell about Frey. Even Old Crotchety was off for Thanksgiving and a substitute nurse was on duty. I tried to tell her what had happened as we walked down the hall back to our ward.

Frey was still lying on his bed with the earphones on when we came in.

"Hi," I called from the doorway.

"One time."

He didn't cry. He was listening to the radio.

"How are you doing?" I said, and I know there was pain in my voice.

Frey just smiled at me. I turned away and almost cried. I was really upset, because for a moment, I had been in a window of some kind in some other place with Frey. For a few moments, he had been free from his stroke. His words spoken to me had been clear and distinct. If I had been able to run, I believe I would have run outside, trying to catch up to that moment that had been lost. I would have caught up to it so I could bring it back to Frey. It was incredible. Shivers went up and down my spine.

Next morning I told Doc Wilson, and all he could do was shake his head, too. It was so weird, maybe he thought I was just a bit nuts. I didn't talk much about it after that, but I know it happened. For a moment, I had seen Frey free from, "One time."

The experience haunted me, and I woke up in the middle of the night with it on my mind. I couldn't shake it, so I went out to the sunporch and worked for more than an hour between the parallel bars. I almost expected something weird to pop up in the mirror while I was working out.

I really wondered why the situation couldn't be recreated or reenacted. If it worked once, why wouldn't it work again? I mean, Frey lying there with his earphones on, relaxed and free from the tension of the stroke. I tried my idea out on Zim the next day, but he didn't hear me, and all I got out of him was, "Humph."

After that I decided to forget it as far as trying to do something about it was concerned. I've never forgotten it. I kept myself very busy with exercises for the next few days, and Thursday that week at swimming I darned near killed Swede trying to score a goal. Even Russian found me a bit more pesky on the wrestling mats than usual, but he still had no trouble handling me. He was strong.

It was about this time after Thanksgiving that Russian began to play around with a ward newspaper called, "Russian's Review." He proceeded to use it for the purpose of taking a look at life around the hospital from a nonfarmer's point of view. It was often an overview of farmers and was usually noncomplimentary to those patients.

"A lot of 'dung' farmers around here," was one of his lines. Only Russian and I were non-farmers in our group. He also wrote, "A lot of farmers pushed dirt around with their noses."

It was not exactly clear what he meant by that, but one thing was clear. He certainly didn't make any extra friends in the farming community by his remarks. Also, his reference to "Our fallen angels with wings held high in splints" was not overlooked or misunderstood. Thus, the cornpicker patients were also included as targets of his barbs.

He was salty, and his dislike for Zim was obvious in this comment, "If we are to have law and order in this hospital situated on government property, the first thing we have to do is take out all the head PT therapists and stretch them out like hot dogs."

Old Crotchety fared no better with Russian, "If we are to have tenderness and compassion during our nighttime hours—when we are in our most extreme pain and loneliness—then our night nurses with advance tenure ought not be cast in concrete. We need softness, not rigidity; sweet breath, not garlic fog."

And again, "If we are to enjoy peaceful repose during the night, free from professional snoring, then all World War I patients ought to be segregated in wards away from World War II patients."

He went back again against Old Crotchety and the other night nurses:

"All night nurses ought to return to wearing masks, as they are now scaring the bejabbers out of us when they flash their flashlights in our faces in the middle of the night to see if we are asleep. Sometimes looking back at them is so upsetting, it is downright difficult to get back to sleep."

Russian followed up on this editorial comment with a connecting thought:

"All Castor Oil dispensations ought to be accompanied by:

1. A soft sheet liner across the center of the bed in anticipation of an unforseen accident occurring due to a too active effect of the oil.
2. Diapers.
3. And no comments."

Further bodily needs included: "We need and want softer toilet paper, particularly those of us who have trouble with our plumbing departments. If we were women patients, we would have had it long ago."

"All haircuts done in the hospital ought to be done by veterans. All G.I. haircuts should be banned on account of we are sensitive."

An insight into some of the horseplay still going on came with: "Saltier crackers are needed for our evening snacks because if they happen to be used in conjunction with a designated short sheet affair approved by the ward, they will be more effective in making the target patient uncomfortable in a more immediate span of time."

And finally, a longing for the good old days came through loud and clear with this quip: "We want our fold-up wheelchairs back so we can demonstrate we are responsible as we know we are. Doc Wilson could make some friends if he does."

Trudy had found Russian some kind of mimeograph duplicator on which he could also draw. So, in addition to slanted editing or reporting, depending on how one looked at it, we were also exposed to Russian art. We could hardly tell what the pictures were supposed to be. Somehow, Russian got to do this project during Trudy's OT time in the afternoon. Distribution was free. I think Trudy saw

Russian needed some encouragement, as there wasn't much doing in his leg development. He did overlook one important aspect of this early newspaper experience: he had no "Letters to the Editor" space available.

CHAPTER EIGHTEEN

Milestones

During this time, around Thanksgiving, I was working on my chenille rug. I had already finished a bedspread of the same material on the floor loom. It was beautiful material. Nothing was too good for the V.A. at that time. I was now working the shuttle with both feet without the use of my hands, lifting up my right leg to successfully push down on the foot lever to move the shuttle.

Other signs of improvement were showing up all over the place as the days went by after Thanksgiving. I was walking to chow regularly and carrying my own tray. I was proud of being able to carry my own tray over to the table from the cafeteria line. As my walking came back, balance became a spooky thing, but I was getting it. One more reason to feel more confident. Swede told me learning to balance was a big thing for him, too. We were both making progress. I noticed that some kinds of music from the dining hall loud speakers seemed to interfere with my balance.

I could walk clear down to PT now and back without falling down once. I didn't make it 100 percent every day, but falling was the exception now. In the swimming pool, I continued to make progress in my tiptoe ability. I was down to waist deep for my right foot and down to just above knee deep for my left leg. That was on the third step coming into the pool. Water polo was still a thing apart from all the rest of the things we did together.

There came a day when Zim replaced Rex at water polo while Rex worked with Onion. On this day, it seemed as though Russian gave up all thought of scoring a goal and concentrated on trying to drown Zim. After a while it became obvious what Russian was trying to do. The rest of us felt uneasy, but Zim held his own and did not lose his temper. I think the Russian scow released a large load of anger that day, and I think Zim was way ahead of the skipper in knowing what was going on.

But we did have one mishap at the swimming pool that day. It happened while we were taking our showers. Onion was sitting in his collapsible chair, the water streaming down on him, when all of a sudden the hot water shut off and we were all zapped with straight cold water. Ed moved right out on his Canadian sticks, Swede grabbed his crutches and got out. I escaped and then turned to hear Onion at his very best.

He wasn't loud, but he was clear and sharp, and the words coming out of his mouth were something never to be equalled as the cold water continued to shower down on him. He was scathing. Judging from the tone of his words, he wasn't nearly so cold as the water was. Rex got to him shortly, but it must have seemed like an eternity to Onion. His skin was pink.

"Rex, I thought you were my friend."

"I am."

"What took you so long?"

"I got to you as quickly as I could. Was it cold on you?"

"I couldn't feel a thing. It's the polio you know. I don't feel much. I just wanted to see you guys move."

There was a big grin on Onion's face.

Back at the hospital, more milestones appeared. Zim got Putzie up on crutches, worked him hard at balancing, and in a week turned him over to Canadian sticks. Putzie was elated, his round face a bundle of smiles. Out of that happy face came a startling sound, "Quack, quack, quack, quack."

I looked at Putzie in astonishment, but he said, "I do that when I get excited. I've done it for a long time. Quack quack, quack quack."

Then he giggled and took another step on his sticks. But he still hadn't arrived. As yet, no beer. His catheter had given him an infection, and it was a long time healing. So even without the catheter, he still waited for his beer and he still couldn't go swimming with us. But he was walking on his sticks, and he was happy. He was engaged in stretching out his milestones.

"You know," he said, "I sure hate what Zim did to me, stretching my hamstrings and lower back muscles, but I needed what he did to me. He's good at what he's doing here. I honestly think he must have written the book on our kind of PT."

"Changing your attitude about Zim?" asked Russian.

"Well, I am. Times change, and I'm feeling better."

Meantime, Ed set himself a goal which he called "Doing my mile."

On his Canadian sticks, he walked clear down the hall to the reception desk and back again. His first round trip took him 15 minutes. We celebrated on the 10th of December when he did it in just five minutes, striding with the sticks and swinging out his legs. He had developed a rhythm that certainly had him moving. Then he told us about a new project he had been working on in private.

"I go downstairs backwards. It works for me. I've been practicing and I haven't fallen down once. It scares me when I get to the top of some stairs and look way down there to the bottom and think about trying to drop my sticks down a step or two without falling down head over heels, don't you know? But if I turn around and slide a foot down to the next step, one at a time while I'm leaning forward towards the steps, I feel right comfortable not looking way down, don't you know?"

It wasn't Ed's habit to smile much. But there was no doubt that he was pleased with his progress and his ability to reason out how he was going to get over the hurdles placed in his life by polio.

It was about the first week of December that Putzie reached another milestone. He had his first beer since the one he had had way back at the Wayne County Fair. Some of his relatives came down from up north and took Putzie out for a while. I was pleasantly surprised when he returned with this big grin on his face. I could tell he wanted me to ask him what was going on. He couldn't keep it in any longer.

"Quack quack, quack quack."

"Okay, Putzie, you look more like an owl than a duck. What's going on?"

"I had a beer. I had a beautiful, precious, delicious, and completely satisfying beer. You are looking at one fulfilled person. I wanted another but my folks said they had promised Doc Wilson only one this time. But I had a beer. It was almost a holy event. I feel almost complete again. Oh, it tasted good, so good."

Something else involving Doc Wilson was going on that indicated another kind of easing of restrictions. There was a gradual eroding of his decree that we were to have no fast wheelchairs. We were careful at first so as not to attract attention, but gradually after each Thursday afternoon swimming session at the Y and our return to the PX in our fancy fold-up wheelchairs, one or two of them managed to make it back up to the wards. They would be ours for a day or two before being returned to the maintenance room. Then mysteriously, in another day or two, they would be upstairs again.

There were always some of the old-fashioned, front-wheel wooden wheelchairs around so Doc Wilson could always see that they were there.

This was high-level, joint strategy for us, and we seemed to handle the transition back to the flashy wheelchairs without danger. Doc Wilson never said a word, but we were much more careful in the hallways. There were no more accidents, but one of the two traveling medicine carts with all the test tubes and jiggly stuff was accidently buzzed again by Russian. It was a near fatal crash right in the center hall. Safe, but oh, so close.

I knew I was getting close to getting out of the hospital. My progress was beginning to show. All those hours in front of the full-length mirror between the parallel bars were obviously paying off. I knew I was going to make it now. It was only a matter of time. Attitude had everything to do with walking again. I wanted to walk again. I wanted to walk again more than anything else, and I had put my mind to it. I was getting control of my hip flopping out. About the only weakness I couldn't master was the slap foot on my left leg. I still had to have the garter rigged up with the spring to the shoe to let my foot down easy. I hated it, but I needed it.

Doc Wilson decided he wanted to see how well I could do on an overnight all by myself away from the hospital. I think he wanted to see how well I would do, not only physically but emotionally and socially as well. I had been hospitalized for over four months, so I was going to take a shot at yet another kind of rehabilitation. Could I fit back in? I was scared and I was excited.

When he suggested my going on an overnight, I thought about asking Long Legs out for a few drinks and some R and R. I told her what the plan was. Maybe she even knew and was in on it, but she seemed both receptive and cooperative. After I made a Saturday night reservation at a local downtown hotel, Long Legs said, "I'll give you a ride to the hotel in the late afternoon since I have to come out here to get some things anyway. After I drop you off at the hotel, I'll come back in the evening for some drinks and conversation. That will be nice."

That sounded more than nice to me.

I planned not to carry my suitcase as I didn't think I could manage it. I just took my ditty bag with my toilet articles in it. I planned on sleeping in my underwear. At the hotel desk, the manager asked me, "Do you have a bag, sir?"

"No," I said, "I'm traveling light; I just have my ditty bag."

He gave me a sharp side glance. A glance of utter disdain. It seemed to say that my not having a suitcase was more than a bit strange if not vulgar. I felt that he was trying to make me feel guilty. I wasn't measuring up to his standards. Then he rang the desk bell and called, "Front!"

When the bellboy came up, the manager said to him, "Take Mr. Hall up to 313. He has no luggage other than his ditty bag."

The way he said "ditty bag" just wreaked with contempt. I knew I was being tried, but so far, I wasn't angry or afraid.

For an instant, the bellboy couldn't decide whether or not he should carry the ditty bag. I was ready to hand it to him if he wanted it. I was sort of cradling it in both hands in front of me. Our eyes met, and I could tell he wasn't sure of himself either. He couldn't tell whether or not I was trying to protect my ditty bag or give it to him. His indecision soon gave way to action. He decided not to carry my ditty bag and so led me to the elevator with, "This way, sir."

I found myself feeling nervous as I began going up in the elevator with the bellboy. It was absolutely quiet as we started up. I looked down at my shoes. They needed polishing. I couldn't do anything about that. I thought of whistling but didn't. I don't think he could have handled that. At least my finger nails were clean so I didn't have to pick at them. I was glad I wasn't wearing that garter and spring attachment on my left leg. I think I would have died of embarrassment if I had had to wear it, yet my foot was slapping enough to be noticed. As the silence lengthened, I looked up over the door to watch the numbers go from M to 2 to 3. It was not a fast elevator. At last, the door opened and the bellboy showed me to room 313 and gave me my key. I tipped him a quarter. I hoped that was right. He said, "Thank you, sir," and left.

So far, I had been steady on my feet. I pulled back the curtain and looked out the window. I could see lights in the other wing of the hotel and in the dusk could dimly make out an alley running across the back of the hotel. I had a bathroom with tub and shower, towels and drinking glasses. There was a Gideon's Bible in the top center drawer of the desk along with some writing paper with the "Cornhusker Hotel" letterhead. I looked at the phone and thought, "The only person I know in town is Long Legs and it's too early for her to call."

That really wasn't true. I could have called Zim or Rex or anyone else I knew from the hospital, but I didn't think it would be okay to call them, particularly so late on a Saturday evening. I thought to myself, "I'd better go down to the coffee shop and get something to eat before I get the blues."

This time on the elevator, there was a middle-aged couple talking, so I didn't feel too uncomfortable as we went down. I didn't feel they were paying any attention to me, so I didn't have to worry about my unpolished shoes or check my finger nails. I was content to watch the number, and as soon as the door opened on the main floor, I headed for the coffee shop.

I went to a seat at the counter and quickly found myself amused and interested in reading the menu. There were all kinds of different foods I hadn't been eating for a long time. I told the waitress, "I'll have a cheeseburger, French fries and a chocolate malt."

"We just have milk shakes."

"That's fine."

I wished I had a newspaper or a magazine to read while I was waiting for my order to come. Since I didn't, I tried to strike up a conversation with an older man dressed in nice clean bib overalls seated in the chair next to me. I opened with, "Do you live here in Lincoln?"

"Nope, I'm from Ord."

"Oh," I said, and for some reason, I found myself feeling disappointed. Besides, I couldn't remember where Ord was, but I remember friends talking about the good pheasant hunting near Ord so it was probably west and north.

"Do you live here in Lincoln?" he asked me this time.

"No, I'm a patient out at the hospital."

"Which hospital?" he quickly asked.

"The Veterans Hospital."

He seemed to relax some when he heard my answer.

"Get hit during the war?"

"No, I'm getting over a case of polio."

This information seemed to tighten him up a second time.

"Polio, is it? That's terrible stuff. Is it catching?"

"I don't really know and I don't think the doctors know either. But I know I'm about over mine. Hope to be out of the hospital in another week or two. They're letting me out for an overnight here at the hotel to see how well I can do for myself. They want to see if I'm ready to be released."

"You look okay to me. Where did it get you?"

"Mostly in my legs, but I can walk pretty well now."

"Well, I hope you make it."

The waitress brought him his dinner and he seemed glad for the diversion to break off our conversation. He went back to reading his newspaper while he ate. Not too long afterwards, my food came too.

The cheeseburger looked beautiful and tasted even better. I thoroughly enjoyed a good ol' American meal. The milk shake was made with ice cream right out of our midwestern dairy country.

It was delicious. I paid for my meal, tipped the waitress and said, "Good-bye" to the man from Ord. I looked around the lobby but didn't see Long Legs, so I went back up to my room and waited for her to call. It seemed like a long time before the phone rang.

"I'm in the lobby."

"I'll be right down."

I hoped I didn't sound too eager. She melted me by looking so alluring in her light blue sweater. The easy way she fitted into it was nearly perfect. It was not tight, so it communicated softness beneath.

"Hi," I said, "You look great!"

"Flattery will get you nowhere."

"But you really do look great. I'm glad you came down. Is the bar here okay?"

"Not bad. Nice quiet atmosphere, but a bar is a bar."

"Let's try it," I said, glad for the chance at a place close at hand instead of hiking some distance. She took my arm as we went in. Her touch this time was altogether different from her touch at the hospital when she might be helping me up or handing me the volleyball. I felt a tingle at her touch.

We found a booth in a semi-lighted corner. There was a candle burning in a little globe on the table. I wouldn't say she was beautiful, but she was very attractive and very desirable right there on the other side of the table. She looked even softer now, and while I couldn't see those beautiful long legs under the table, I could sense their presence.

Then, our knees touched slightly, and I was on fire. I was very much alive and very glad of it. And I was glad that the nerve endings in my legs had come back as well as they had, for they were telling me something essential about Long Legs' closeness. She ordered a screwdriver and I ordered rye and water.

"What's a Screwdriver?" I asked after the waiter left.

"It's a lady's drink with orange juice in it. How are you doing?"

"I'm doing okay. I'm a little nervous, but I'm glad you're here. Makes me feel better."

I told her about dinner and the man from Ord.

"Sounds like you're doing fine."

"I like being with you."

"I like being with you too on your first night out of the hospital. And we're doing the right thing. We're celebrating."

I wanted to get much closer to her than sitting across the table but didn't know how. Knee touching was stirring me more than I cared to know. We talked about the hospital and all the people there, and that was good for two drinks. Then she got going about a favorite cousin who lived in Los Angeles. Long Legs went on and on about how she loved to visit there, and that was good for one more drink. I began to feel no pain.

As I became more relaxed, I grew bolder, and so at a lull in the conversation, I said, "Do you know you have very good looking legs? And do you further know that we all call you Long Legs at the hospital because you show off your legs so well to us so often?"

"Thank you. I aim to please. That's my job."

I didn't want to hear the slight emphasis she put on the word "job," because I found myself saying, "You surely please me and I wouldn't mind at all being pleased lots more by you."

"I think you are a nice guy. A real nice guy and interesting, too. I've never been out with anyone who drinks rye and water."

"Want a sip?"

"No, thanks. And I don't want to confuse business with pleasure. You see, my being here with you is half business and half pleasure. And I really am enjoying myself with you this way. I like being friends with you. That's the pleasure half."

"That's nice," I said. "And that's as far as it goes?"

"Look," she said, "I can probably drink you right under this table. I've got a hollow leg as they say in the trade."

"A very beautiful one indeed. Which one is it?"

Long Legs pulled back a little from the table, perhaps thinking I might try reaching under the table to find out which was her hollow leg. Our knee contact was broken. I was painfully aware of the separation. Then she went on, "I'm just going to sit here with you. Nothing else is going to happen except perhaps you'll get more tipsy."

"How is it that you have such a steel trap for a mind? How can you stay in such control? And yet, showing off your long, oh, such good-looking legs, seems to be saying something else."

"Oh, I show all of you patients my long legs to perk you guys up. Gives you something else to think about. You see, while you were getting your degree from Yale, I was matriculating at the school of hard knocks. I've had to learn how to get on in life by using my wits. I don't know about you, but most of the lessons I've learned in life I learned the hard way. But I learn them well.

"So I've learned that when a guy wants to get real cozy and has ideas, if my first excuse isn't good enough, my third or fourth one will be. I must look out for myself much the same way you do. I admire you for the way you keep at it between the parallel bars in front of that full-length mirror. You've got what it takes. Let's be friends and have one more drink and call it a night. You're doing fine, but your head won't feel so good in the morning."

We had a last drink, and Long Legs gave me a peck on the cheek in the lobby as she said good-night to me. What a warm woman! I savored my time with her, for I was convinced that I was taking a step back into the mainstream of life. All the same, I was most frustrated. Those long legs haunted me.

CHAPTER NINETEEN

Good-bye

The next morning, I had a mild hangover that I almost enjoyed. After all, Zim had told me I had to learn how to deal with all kinds of pain and even conquer it. What was his line? Pain is a natural phenomenon, misery is optional. So it was with me this morning. The pain in my head and my longing for Long Legs. Not too bad a combination of pain to deal with.

I stayed in bed late in the morning. What a big change from the hospital routine. I had a late morning breakfast that really turned out to be a brunch; scrambled eggs, hashbrowned potatoes, bacon, toast, jam, orange juice, and coffee. It was good coffee. I took my time and enjoyed it, and I knew I was enjoying it.

I took a bus over to the capitol and walked around there for a while and felt pretty good. Even went clear up to the top of the skyscraper part of the capitol for a view of the whole city and the surrounding prairie. I could clearly see the V.A. Hospital far below a mile or two away. That's where my comrades were. During the months we had been there, we had come to share so much so closely together. We knew a great deal about each other, good and bad, strengths and weaknesses. We had suffered and shared together. We had supported one another, and a loyalty had developed amongst us. We counted on each other. We were a close knit group.

This was my homeland where my six friends came from. Nebraska had been my family's home since the earliest of pioneer days. From early childhood, I had heard the litany of family exploits extolling our pioneer ancestors. Eventually, I became part of the tradition.

Not too far away from where I was, Black Elk, the Sioux Medicine Man, had given me a blessing in the Dakota language when he put his hands on my head. I was nine years old and I remember his voice sounding like a swift flowing mountain stream gurgling over hidden boulders as his voice rose and fell in his chant-like way of speaking. I remember when I looked up at him, he seemed to have a big nose. I had his ceremonial moccasins tucked away somewhere.

Where I was standing was close to where chief Logan Fontonelle of the Omaha tribe had been ambushed almost a hundred years ago by a roving band of Sioux. Shortly before his death, he had told my great-grandfather he would take many Sioux with him. Supposedly, he did. Those stories of my ancestors ran deep. Likewise, my roots were growing deeper into this prairie land by way of my struggle against polio with my friends. No one needed to tell me that I had been doing some powerful living those last few months. I had lived up to my family's traditions by making my own contribution.

I had long-time friends not too far away in Omaha, and now new and very important friends down there in the hospital. We were all from Nebraska. This was where I fitted in. I liked knowing that.

Down below me was the nameplate of the county—named after my great-grandfather—carved in stone at the northwest corner of the capitol. My roots went down deep in the prairie soil.

This time of reflection was important to me. I had been so busy getting well, I hadn't taken much time to think about what was next. Now, I had time to appreciate what had happened to me. It was as though I could drink it all in from up there on top of the capitol building and make some order out of my therapy. Find some understanding to my life. I felt assured. I felt strong.

I knew I had won a victory over fear after much hard work and agony shared with my friends, but I don't think I was capable then of saying, "I feel anxious." I simply wasn't that much in touch with my feelings, and I don't think I can lay my numbness at the feet of my polio. It went back further than that to my rescuing business.

I am sure now that I didn't know whether or not I was angry about my legs being bad. But this time of contemplation was special time for me, and I was glad to have it even if some things weren't coming out clearly. I did know I was moving along.

The sky was gray, streaked with darker clouds riding fast on a gusty fall wind. It was dismal and haunting. I seemed to be almost high enough to touch those clouds from the top of the capitol. Far below, the wind swirled the fallen leaves across the spacious dark green lawn. I could distinctly hear their far-away dry rattle as they were caught by the wind in bending waves weaving across the grass.

Then a feeling of sadness filled me. There was a sadness to my leaving the hospital, although, of course, it was my goal. It was a tremendously important part of my life that I was literally about to walk away from. As the blowing leaves marked the end of the season, so too, their action seemed to be signaling my changing time.

I watched, and then, since there was no one else at the top with me, I felt free to let my feelings flow. I soared on the wind of my sadness by whistling the tune "Shenandoah":

"Oh Shenandoah, I long to see thee
Away you rolling river,
It's been seven long years
Since last I see thee,
Away, away, away, away,
Across the wide Missouri."

Those were the words I could remember. From where I was, I couldn't quite see the Missouri River to the east, but it was close. I had grown up on that river in Omaha, and this was the Shenandoah, across the wide Missouri.

My six comrades there in the hospital, and some of the staff were part of the mix cementing my strong feeling of belonging in my Shenandoah. Our friendships were anchored in genuine pain and gutsy living, and we were very much alive. I knew I had been living at the courage and patience level with my friends.

But now, it was time to go. I had to be moving on as the leaves were below. At the moment, I didn't know anymore where I was going than where the leaves were going, but the surge in me to move on was strong.

I came down, grabbed a taxi and returned to the hospital in time for our Sunday afternoon snack.

Naturally, all the guys wanted to know how I made out on my overnight. I didn't disappoint them with my usual service-type banter.

"You should have seen all those beautiful women in the lobby of the hotel. I had to fight to keep them off me. Swede, you wouldn't have had a chance with your weak arm. But I stood firm and took them one at a time."

After that overnight, I began to make plans for my release. Before I left, I had to finish the scarf I was making on a small loom for Rich Young. It was a Black Watch plaid made of the finest wool, and counting all the different colors and weaving them in correctly by the numbered pattern I had designed was an arduous task of love for me. The scarf was almost four feet long.

My good-bye to my friends and the staff at the hospital came the day before Christmas. The day before my departure, we held our Christmas party on the sunporch, and it became a meaningful farewell. A change of pace from the regular routine provided a good sharing atmosphere for me to say good-bye.

PART IV
Sunny, Stormy, Cloudy and Rainbows

CHAPTER TWENTY

My Tale

I hated wearing the garter on my left leg with the spring to my shoe to let my slap foot down nice and easy. I was embarrassed by it. I soon got rid of it with lots more exercise. One permanent result of polio is that I've kept up my exercises. I went to Chicago for brokerage training and lived on the near north side. I didn't want a slap foot in that fast crowd. Within a year, I was able to walk almost without a limp, but I have always had difficulty going up stairs.

After I came back to the Omaha branch office, I soon became a major producer for the company. In a few years, I married the boss' secretary from Chicago. She was used to making regular golf appointments for her boss with Ike at Augusta and was a star secretary. But we soon found ourselves in a very unhappy marriage. We stuck it out for seventeen years. Since I had shut off my feelings, I had a hard time understanding hers. My iron will got in the way too. That's the one that kept me going between those parallel bars.

Instead of taking an honest look at ourselves, we moved to California, and I started a new business. I was aching for answers to my unhappiness. I came in contact with a number of young Episcopal priests in the diocese of California. Some of them seemed to have something I was missing.

I decided I needed to find God, so I went to the local seminary and studied to become an Episcopal priest. I ate up loads and loads of information about God and the Bible, but I don't think I became very well acquainted with a loving God. Yet in my agony, I was making headway in that direction.

During a retreat with my class, I found myself searching back through my polio experience. I was looking to see if I could understand myself better. I found something else. With some help, I began to appreciate the place Rich Young had played in my life and, most particularly, in my recovery.

He was the one who wrote the piece in *Mental Hygiene* about the anxiety of polio patients and their family members. As I began to recover, I had asked him about polio, and he gave me the article that he had written, along with several other informative pieces. But what he did for me was a great deal more than intellectual stimulation. He had simply poured out his life for me. I could appreciate this now in a new way because of my religious studies, but I was also experiencing some gut level response to his love as well.

He must have sensed that it was a time in my life when I was agnostic. I simply didn't believe. He probably knew that I was not praying and had no consciousness of God looking after me and protecting me. Even in the midst of all that terror, I had made no approach to a God who might comfort me. I don't think I would have known how to pray, but that was certainly the time when I might have begun.

Now, ten years later, on a retreat with my class from seminary, I began to share with my Bishop some of the thoughts and feelings I could recollect from my polio experience. I began to be aware of some deep feelings coming to the surface, and anger seemed to be the strongest emotion I was able to identify.

I said to my Bishop, "It seems to me that this would have been the time for God to make Himself known to me. I was broken in body and spirit so I was ready for him. I was in as much misery as I have ever experienced in my entire life. It seems to me that this would have been the time for God to have made Himself known to me. I was desperate. I was broken. Why didn't He make His presence known? Why wasn't that my time?"

Though my Bishop had been listening carefully, he did not seem defensive in the face of my aggressive questioning. "I don't know what to say to you, Bob. Why don't you tell me more about your experience?"

So I did. And I told him about Rich Young. By the time I finished, his chuckles were turning into outright laughter, and I could feel myself bristling.

"Well," he said, "God was indeed with you all the way through."

"What do you mean God was with me all the way through? There was no Bible, there were no prayers, no sacrament, no . . ."

"Your doctor? Dennis?" my Bishop broke in.

"Every time your doctor came shuffling down the ward, God

came with him to see you. Where do you suppose his courage and love came from? Where do you think Dennis' patience came from? There was all kinds of God's love sustaining you. What do you think Metch was talking about? Maybe you think you should have received some kind of vision. Well, you did. A real one. "Your doctor was real. Dennis was real. I find God in people. You did too. They gave you what you needed in that hospital. It made sense to you. You were comforted. I would say you were blessed through them. You weren't ready to comprehend God's presence in a religious way at that time. Look at how you rejected the Bible that was given you.

"Eventually, it did get used at the right time, but the right time wasn't then. Everything has its own time. It's just taken you some time to recognize the real thing."

I was no longer the same person I had been earlier. I had heard my Bishop and understood my life better. I began to see what had happened to me. Very simply put, the polio event had not only been my initiation into practicing patience, it had been for me, my unspoken God-event. Other people have their times of being "born again" or having a conversion experience, but my time of coming into God's realm was not a dramatic event. It was gradual.

In the County Hospital, I had been in the midst of a life and and death struggle. It had been a crisis, and in that extraordinary setting, I had been absorbing God's presence through the imposition of practicing patience. I understand this process of absorbing God's holiness in much the same manner as a frog drinks water. It does not lap it up but, rather, sits in the water and absorbs it into its system through the pores of its skin. Likewise, I had been absorbing patience from Dennis, Rich Young, Metch and Bobby. Later, I absorbed it from Zim when I got up 36 times on my way to PT.

What a subtle shift this unrecognized growing in God had been for me, moving me away from relying mostly upon my intellectual approach to life so well developed at Yale.

Patience always gives me power. It works. It allows enough time for love and compassion. Patience is best in lovemaking. Patience allows me to think clearly. Allows me to savor the moment. It is a virtue in the mirror of truth. Patience is a blessing.

Not too many people are patient. We, as polio patients, didn't learn it once and for all and then were done with it. None of us "arrived" with patience, but we found a new depth to living as we practiced it. I still grow today as I practice patience.

I graduated from seminary and became a parish priest in the Episcopal Church. After my divorce, I became a worker priest and went back into the investment business. I remarried and spent ten of the happiest years of my life in a team ministry with my wife. We had a neat house in the country, about a mile away from one of our churches. Then, a tragedy engulfed our marriage, and I went through pain even greater than the polio pain. I agonized through my second divorce.

That was when I joined the support group called Adult Children of Alcoholics (ACA). My counselor had shown me that I came from an alcoholic household where the disease went back several generations. I had no trouble with the drink, but I found out I did with the disease. It was quite a revelation when I learned I had followed the classic pattern of a person growing up in a dysfunctional family by becoming a rescuer. That's when I also learned that my great-grandfather, who had given his name to that county in Nebraska, had died of alcoholism at age forty-nine.

Through my group work, I'm getting in touch with some of those feelings that were trying to get out when I was recovering from polio. I'm growing stronger, and patience becomes a more important part of my life. When I practice it, life is great, and when I don't, life is the pits. In group sharing, I've found many similarities in recovery between polio and alcoholism. Hope and patience are major similarities. One of our slogans is, "Don't push the river, let it flow by itself." I'm beginning to see some blue sky around me, and I like it.

CHAPTER TWENTY-ONE

Reunion

By June of 1950, our group had left the hospital at Lincoln. Onion was the last to leave. For a while, several members kept in touch. Ed and Bernice lived at Lynch, just north of the Niobara River in northern Nebraska. They would visit Russian in Omaha when Ed came down to the V.A. Hospital for checkups. Russian often took his boys camping up north on the Niobara and so stayed in touch with Ed and Bernice for a while. Ed and Swede saw Spook a couple of times at Burwell on the edge of the Sandhills, and once Ed and Bernice stopped to visit Onion on his farm near Mason City in central Nebraska.

When I moved to Chicago, I lost touch with the group except for Putzie. After I returned to Omaha, Putzie stopped by on his way home to Pilger. He was walking around on Canadian sticks with some difficulty. He had become too heavy. His beer showed up all over him. He was carrying around at least 225 pounds, up 65 pounds from his weight at the hospital.

He seemed happy, as was his nature, so why worry about a little weight? We had a good, but short, visit. He had gone to watch repair school in Kansas City for two years and was then trying to make a living at watch repairing at Pilger.

From then on, we kept in touch by messages on our Christmas cards, and I noted his marriage in 1963. His cards were happy until a few years ago when one came telling of his wife's death. He seemed to go downhill after that and about seven years ago, I lost track of him.

In January of 1985, when I was back in Omaha on a combination business and pleasure trip, I looked in the phone book to see if Russian was listed. He was. I called him, and he answered. I hadn't talked to Russian in 35 years. Suddenly, it seemed as if those years were gone. His voice sounded the same when he said, "Sure, Bob, come on out. I'll be glad to see you."

I found him living in a comfortable mobile home with a mechanical lift at the door for getting him in and out in his wheelchair. He looked good. Hadn't changed much in 35 years. His handgrip almost broke my hand.

"Bob, we made it!"

I didn't quite understand what he meant.

"I mean we all made it. Even Onion. Even he was able to make a living and make a success out of living. No welfare. No charity, no help the handicapped. We all made it! We made it all by ourselves!"

I was immediately caught up by his intensity more than I was by his words. I found myself deeply moved by seeing Russian, and I was interested in what he was saying. Many feelings were surging through me all at once and I was having difficulty sorting them out.

It was obvious that he had kept in touch with the rest of the group. Almost immediately, I was moved to suggest that we have a reunion. That was fine with him. I hadn't even thought about a reunion before seeing Russian, but all of a sudden, it seemed the only natural thing to do. Russian had all the addresses, and I had a WATS line. After a most pleasant visit we started to plan it, probably at the V.A. Hospital in Lincoln.

From our visit, I learned that Russian had lived a lively life as labor negotiator for his union. He worked as a precision grinder at Viccars, a big factory in Omaha, but his writing skills had quickly involved him in the publishing of the weekly union newsletter. From there, he had become involved in labor-management relations and bargaining. He was good at it, but it led to traveling. Therein came some problems, as he tried to negotiate off and on airplanes with crutches rather than his wheelchair. He was close to his kids and, during his early years, had been instrumental in having a multi-playing field complex for youngsters built on the growing, north side of Omaha.

Russian had told me that all the group still lived in Nebraska except for me. It was a good day's drive for me from the Twin Cities where I lived, but the reunion could be done over a weekend. Maybe I could fly down to Omaha and ride with Russian. We would see.

I had never been to a reunion of any kind in my life, so I found myself getting excited about having this one. After all these years, we were actually going to get back together. Seeing Russian and listening to him tell me how we all had made it through life, each on his own, was a moving experience. Even Onion had made it, getting by on his farm. Russian had explained that Onion had a V.A. pension, and his wife Charlotte did most of the farm work. The kids pitched in enough to help on their irrigated farm to make it go. Russian had also told me that Putzie was in the Vets home at Norfolk, Nebraska. That must have been when I lost track of him. Russian and I started out planning for the reunion to be at the V.A. Hospital at Lincoln. However, a few phone calls changed all that.

Max Lybarger, the director of the Lincoln V.A. Hospital was most responsive when I called him with our idea of a reunion. "You are most welcome to come here for a weekend but the place more or less shuts down from Friday afternoon to Sunday night. We no longer have a cafeteria. All the patients eat in their rooms. Everything has changed. You wouldn't know the place anymore. Your sunporch is long gone. No one you knew here is around. Doc Wilson died. Most of the PT people you mentioned I don't know about or have died. Zim went east and the last that I knew about him, he was at the V.A. Hospital at New Haven, Connecticut."

"New Haven," I said to myself. "That's where Yale is. I wonder if Zim got in with the Yale hospital staff. I'll have to find out."

When I caught up with Putzie in the Vets Home in Norfolk, Nebraska, he told me he was in no shape to travel. He sounded weak and discouraged. I don't think he had any "quack, quack, quack" left in him. I told him we would come see him. That seemed to perk him up a little.

Jerry Schwede, the administrative assistant there, was the most helpful person. He told me he had a nice room on the first floor with tables where we could meet. Right outside was a screened-in gazebo where I could barbecue the steaks I was bringing. There were a couple of charcoal broilers I could use. He sent me a map showing how to get there and a list of the motels that were close.

He did a super job for us, for when he arrived at Norfolk, he had plates, coffee, utensils and whatever we needed during the weekend.

On the phone, I caught up with Swede at his farm in some very fine farm country outside of Stromsburg, Nebraska. I first talked to his wife, Ruth, head nurse of a large nursing home in Stromsburg. Swede sounded as laid back as ever and was delighted to hear we were going to have a reunion. He and Ruth would both come to Norfolk. But he did have some sad news. Onion had died two years previous, but he would contact his widow, Charlotte, to see if she wanted to come.

"Maybe we could pick her up," he offered, "Mason City isn't too far out of the way. Onion just wore out. Died of kidney complications."

That was the only one of our five reunions Charlotte missed. She later told us that Onion had lived much longer than had been expected. His big event had come seven years before he died, when a trucker friend had given him a CB. That event changed his life. He had turned into an angel over the airwaves, bringing rescue to stranded people. He became most helpful in a general way. As we listened, it was obvious that she was telling us something bordering on miraculous.

As we listened to and recorded our reunion stories, it became obvious that in addition to our polio story, there were seven powerful stories of how well we all had coped.

Ed was surprised at first to hear from me when I called him on the phone, and for a while was confused, but he was delighted I was calling. After a short consultation with Bernice, he said, "Count on us. We'll be there."

When we finally set the date, Russian said, "I'll see you up there. I have my own car with special attachments and I'll drive up."

Spook was hard to find at Burwell, Nebraska, a small city on the eastern edge of the Sandhills. It is famous for its rodeos. There was no answer to my phone calls. The post office did say his mail was being forwarded to a place outside the state but they couldn't tell me where. Postal regulations. So I sent him the letter I sent to the rest of the group and told him I hoped he could make it. Swede said he thought Spook had been in the real estate and insurance business. Very big in real estate.

Part of my August 16, 1985, letter to the group said:

"The plan is to have a Saturday Night Barbecue with steaks. Sunday breakfast on the grills provided by the Home in the shelter. We can also have lunch there before we depart on Sunday.

"There is a chance Howard Zimmer might be coming out from Connecticut to join us, which would be just great if he can come. Might give some of us a chance to get even with Zim, particularly Putzie.

"So far, everyone is coming except Spook whom I haven't been able to reach by phone as yet.

"I'm looking forward to seeing you all September 21st and 22nd."

When Russian heard Zim might come, he said, "If Zim comes, I'll punch him in the nose."

Catching up with Zim had not been easy. He had retired and

was living at Milford, Connecticut. He sounded good and somewhat prosperous. Said he had his own sail boat which he sailed quite a bit. He had worked at the V.A. Hospital at New Haven, which was in some way connected to the Yale Medical complex. However, he had found the emphasis at Yale was more on research than on practice and so he had retired early.

His wife Ursula sounded delightful. At first, Zim, like Ed, had a hard time remembering me and the group. After I primed his memory a little by reminding him of stretching Putzie and going swimming with us, he remembered well. He thought seriously about coming out to our reunion. He had some other details to take care of in the Nebraska area so he tried combining the scheduling. In the end, it did not work out for him, and so Russian was spared the exercise of swinging on him.

Zim sent two letters; one to me, the other to the group. His letter to me said in part:

Dear Bob:

Having gone back to my 45th college reunion this year and renewing friendships from so long ago makes me realize how rewarding these get-togethers really are. You guys shared life and death, success and failure in the hospital just as a few years earlier you had also shared life with foxhole buddies. These times shall not be forgotten.

Let me thank you twice. First, for putting this reunion together, and second, for inviting me to join with you in renewing friendships. It was the most meaningful invitation I have ever received.

You fellows were the first mass polio group the hospital ever experienced. Nobody knew too much about the disease or its treatment. We just followed the methods of Sister Kenny from Minneapolis and hoped for the best. What we learned from you fellows helped us greatly when we encountered greater numbers in 1952-53...

Bob, it was nice being remembered. Thank you.

Sincerely,
Howard Zimmer

When we finally came to the reunion at Norfolk, we gathered at the Villa Inn first before going out to see Putzie. As I crossed the Missouri River and came back into Nebraska from the north, I was welcomed loudly on the radio to the land of "Big Red," my old Shenandoah. There was no way of getting away from it. All the radio stations were carrying the football game between Nebraska and Illinois. Nebraska was mashing them.

I was glad to see that Cornhusker football was still thriving in Nebraska. My childhood memories of the football games were still strong. I was glad to be back in my home land.

Swede with his wife, Ruth, and I checked in about the same time in the early afternoon. Ed and Bernice arrived shortly thereafter. At the last minute, Russian was unable to come because his son was ill.

There was much small talk as we all sized each other up. We had all gained weight and it showed, particularly in the middle front. Ed soon proved capable as ever at spinning tales and telling stories and it wasn't long before we seemed to fall in together rather well.

Swede, who walked with a cane, was a successful farmer with a history of hard work. He had received a good return for that work. He was living well. During his early farming days, Swede accomplished some truly heroic physical tasks in order to get his work done. Not many people would have undertaken what he did to overcome his limitations brought on by polio. Of course, Swede has always been a down-to-earth believer, and because he has been, he has succeeded handsomely.

We also learned that when Ed and Bernice weren't running their general store in Lynch up north of the Niobrara River, they were fishing. They did a great deal of fishing and Ed's stories were wonderful. Ed was still on his Canadian sticks, but his outlook on life was remarkable. After listening to him for a while, I would never guess in any way that he was handicapped. Even after five reunions, his stories have not run out, and neither has his enthusiasm for life.

When we found the Vets Home, Putzie was waiting for us. He didn't look too bad but he was having trouble getting his arms up. Plumbing was a big problem for him. We sat around the table and swapped stories and then went out and took some pictures.

As a group, we had done better than average in staying alive. I checked with an insurance actuarial and asked how well we did. I said, "In August of 1949, there were seven of us males between the ages of 22 and 25 in a group in Nebraska. Thirty-six years later, how many of us should still be living?"

His answer was, "Five."

We were ahead by one.

Then I read Zim's letter to the group. It went, in part, as follows:

Dear Polio Alumni
Class of 1949:
   What a surprise to receive a phone call from Bob Hall and learn that you guys were going to have a reunion, and that I was invited. I appreciate that very much. As Bob mentioned one name after the other, the recollections were fuzzy with age. About a week later when

I received the snapshots on the sunporch, names and faces came into clear focus. What memories they brought back. It seemed like six years ago, not thirty-six. From what I hear, each one of you has done well since you left the hospital. I am most pleased to hear this as that is what rehabilitation is all about. Don't concentrate on what has been lost, but rather, learn to make the most of what you have left. You guys deserve plaudits for what you have accomplished. It makes me happy to know that I was able to help you during those difficult times.

Putzie, this is for you. I never did get the polio that you wished on me or any of the other curses that you placed on my head. That is until the last fifteen years. Then it was diabetes, aortic aneurysm, and cancer of the prostate—all treated with satisfactory results. Will you settle for that? . . . As I look at those sunporch snapshots again, you guys look so young. Today, I imagine it's pot bellies, grey hair or no hair.

What you look like on the outside doesn't matter though. It's what's on the inside that counts. Your spirit and determination together with your ability to endure pain were commendable. You had what it took.

I wish you joy, happiness and one hell of a good time as you get together on this reunion. Do yourselves a favor and continue these get-togethers so that your friendships are not forgotten . . .

Best wishes,
Howard Zimmer

Putzie was quick to say that he held no grudges against Zim and wished him well in any illness he might have. He spoke for all of us when he said, "I get around as well as I do thanks to Zim. If he had been easier on us, we probably wouldn't have tried nearly as hard as we did. Sure, he got us mad at him many times, but that was for our own good."

We all agreed that because Zim pushed us as hard as he did, we were doing as well as we were. Ruth said, "You'll never know how lucky you all were to have had Zim. I see people every day in that nursing home where I work, who should be pushed the way Zim pushed you. Instead, they are hardly touched, and so they're just moving toward vegetating. Zim gave you tough love. The term wasn't invented then, but that's what he gave you, tough love. It's hard to give. Not many give it. Judging from his letters, it was hard for him to give it. Praise God he was as firm as he was. He could have not cared."

Bernice agreed, "Zim would be amazed to see how well all of you are getting on. It really is remarkable."

"Yes," said Putzie, "I am grateful that he stretched me and pushed me up on those crutches and on to my Canadian sticks. And when he said, 'Follow me,' I guess I believed Zim, because I did follow him. I followed him on my Canadian sticks. I'm glad I did."

Further reflecting on Zim's letter brought on a conversation about the recurring symptoms of polio appearing in our country. There had been a number of articles in magazines and on TV news programs, indicating that former polio victims were being stricken by the recurrence of the original weaknesses of the disease. It was called the Post Polio Syndrome. Some cases went back to attacks of polio as much as thirty and forty years ago.

"How does that work?" I asked Ruth.

"When you came up with a weak muscle or lost the use of a muscle entirely, Zim had you learn which muscles in your arms or legs you could develop to compensate for the weak or lost muscle. You have all done remarkably well in doing this. Bob, you learned to walk with an entirely different set of muscles than I walk with. Your quadriceps were weakened by your polio so you learned to walk with your hip muscles instead. They work fine for you. The damaged muscles and nerves have been replaced by the other muscles and nerves.

"What can happen to you after a good many years is that these substituting muscles and nerves can wear out by over use. It's not unlike overloading an electric circuit and burning it out by continuous overloading. So in your body, the overloading of the substitute muscles and nerves can eventually lead to a resulting burnout. This process can bring on the symptoms of polio again without the disease itself actually taking place.

"A leg begins to drag because a worn out nerve can't get the messages through anymore and so the overloaded muscle grows weak and dries up. This is called atrophy as you all know. Many similar polio symptoms come, but no disease. It appears to me, you have all done very well and have stayed free from these complications. I believe you all have done so well because you had such excellent original treatment."

We reflected on that until Putzie said, "You know, I have lots of time to think in this place because there just isn't all that much for me to do. Not that I'm in any shape to do many things. But I've thought about this disease we've all had. I think we've learned some good lessons from polio, and my biggest lesson is patience."

"I've wondered about that myself," I said, delighted with this confirmation that my recent thoughts about patience were closer to being right on.

"Well, you know," said Ed, "a cynical person might say, 'You had to be patient, what else could you have done?' And he makes an intellectual point, perhaps, but what patience led us into and where it took us was into a new and powerful territory. Makes a fella feel real humble. It isn't easy being humble if that is what a person sets out to do, don't you know.

"Patience smacks of real humility, there's no getting around it. None of us who had polio would ever win a beauty contest or a body beautiful award or excite the excitables by our charm on some TV show, but we had patience. We grew into it at the hospital. We demonstrated its strength by how we worked it out. It's powerful stuff."

"That's right," replied Putzie as he warmed to the subject, "the patience polio demanded from us, and the patience we practiced is in no way a popular mirror to hold up to our society so intent on getting what it wants right now. Our patience stands up against the trend. I know if my hamburger and fries aren't ready in two minutes, I might move my business next door. And if four minutes rolls by, my anger is likely to be my prize.

"I think most of us expect to get whatever we want right now. That's even sicker than being satisfied with getting what I want right now all the time. Do you know what I mean?"

"Yep," said Ed, "it's the expecting part of getting what you want that is so sick. Why, it takes the mystery out of life, as if one of us was actually in charge. Only God is, as far as I know.

"For me, our practice of patience shows there is something else of more value out there in life. It's kind of funny, but our patience was born out of our tenacious effort simply to stay alive. I know for me, out of that effort came a kind of delicacy, a value that added feeling for the very act of being alive. Makes a person grateful.

"Why back at County Hospital, when Rich helped Dennis raise his phlegm in the evening before strapping on his respirator, I'll bet we were all raising our own phlegm and clearing our own throats. Probably thankful too that we could.

"When Rick and Dennis joked about whether or not it had been 'a good one' as Rick wiped the phlegm from Dennis' mouth, their carnal humor seemed almost holy to me. Dennis was so close to not living, and he wanted so powerfully to live. I could just see life was being celebrated right at that moment. Being celebrated by the man with relentless patience."

"You know," said Putzie, "I think we've had something more than good treatment going for us."

The next year, we found that Putzie had delivered some substance to his thought. The change in him between our first and second reunion had been remarkable. At age sixty, he had decided full living was worth the effort. He had been motivated to rise up out of the pit, and his "quack, quack, quack quacks" were back. He relaxed and shared his thoughts with us. "A PT who comes here helped me try one more time. I'm doing exercises, and I can do things I thought I could never do again."

He went on to tell us that most of his life had been spent working as the County Veterans Service Officer and coaching Midgets and Peewees in baseball. He did that until kids of kids he had coached began showing up. Then he knew it was time to hang up the job. A combination of diabetes and arthritis put him in the home. The thing which seemed to please him most was having the baseball playing fields named after him. The community had a plaque dedicated, naming the playing fields after Putzie. We could see that he was pleased, and that made the rest of us enjoy some warm feelings.

We never did enjoy any warm feelings over Spook; he remained a mystery. At our second reunion, we began to learn more about him. I had reached him by phone regarding our second reunion, and he said he would come. He had recently returned to Nebraska from living in Montana, and wanted to see the rest of the group. He didn't come to the reunion, but a patient from the Vet's Home returning from the V.A. Hospital at Grand Island said he had run into Spook there. He was very sick with cancer. Five months later, I reached him at the Grand Island hospital, and he was dying of a large brain tumor. I flew down to see him, spent four hours visiting, and when I left, I still didn't know much about him. He had been too sick, but it did sound as though he had made a lot of money in real estate investments, and then lost most of it. Something sinister happened to him on an airplane once, but that, too, was cloudy and spooky. Spook died seventeen days after I saw him. His death made me sad. We shall miss him at our future reunions.

EPILOGUE

An event occurred during the time of my second marriage when I had become a worker priest and was ministering to two country churches. I was an investment officer in the Investment Services Department in the largest bank in St. Paul, Minnesota. This bank was the principal municipal underwriter in the region. It was a pressure job in a most sophisticated office.

We had a good mix of people in the office, all carefully chosen by a very sharp leader. Our staff included a couple who were real swingers or fancied themselves to be so. During our morning and afternoon coffee breaks, many of us would walk the skywalk to our coffee shop. The traffic was usually heavy along the skywalk, particularly during the winter months, and offered every kind of shop and store imaginable. It was a city within a city, going on for several miles through the heart of St. Paul.

Those two men in our group who fancied themselves swingers also thought they were expert judges of feminine pulchritude as well. Often as we walked along the busy skywalk, these two would provide the rest of us with a running commentary on the more attractive women coming our way; they commented at length on their virtues or lack thereof. They also offered a corresponding high or low esteem assigned to the anatomy in their gaze.

"Boy, look at that one. I'll bet that's not all hers," or "That one looks nice. Seems like she might be real sympathetic to making you feel real cozy. I'd like to try that."

Their carnal attitude reminded me of the professional cattle buyer when viewing a steer and judging quality and weight. As a youngster, I had spent enough time at the large Omaha stockyards to be accustomed to that particular kind of assessment. So it happened one day in the fast-paced setting of the skyways with the two swingers comparing notes on women, that I caught a glimpse of a woman moving briskly down the skyway on Canadian sticks. My breath went short, and I said to myself, "There but for the grace of God, go I."

And the next thing I knew, I was in hot pursuit of her. For some reason, I had to have a look at her face. I didn't know why I felt so strongly that I had to catch up with her to see her face, but I was driven. I quickened my pace through the crowd and shot ahead of the rest of my group heading down for morning coffee.

I could see she had turned the corner and was heading for the big escalator. It went down to our cafe on the first floor where there were big windows looking out on the street. That was where we had coffee. I wanted to see the woman's face; I wanted to see if those two dead legs she was swinging along had put a drag on her face. I needed to see if she was smiling or scowling.

I couldn't believe how fast she was moving. The up and down escalators were long. In between them was the old original white conglomerate marble staircase, shining in the lights. This Stick Lady, as I immediately dubbed her, had chosen to go down the staircase rather than struggle with the crowd on the escalators. She went down two steps at a time without any hesitation. One little slip and she would have been a heap, rolling helplessly down those long stairs. I couldn't believe how quickly she was going down those stairs.

"Bam," went her sticks, and then "whump" came her two dead legs in braces down two more steps. I thought of how careful Ed had gone down stairs backwards to avoid falling. I shuddered. I couldn't catch up with her with the crowd on the escalator. At the bottom of the steps, she went out the revolving doors into a swirl of snow on the street. I reached the bottom of the escalator and raced into the cafe to look out the windows in an effort to see her.

Fortunately, the big windows weren't clouded with condensation from the outside cold even though the cafe was full of people. I was able to see her going by. I felt as though it was meant for me to see her. She was smiling as she went down the street with her cloth book bag over her shoulder. She was smiling. For some unexplainable reason, I was smiling too.

"Thank you, God," I said to myself. "I really appreciate walking. And thank you, God, for that courageous woman."

She seemed so fresh and alive compared to all the BS I had left behind with the group. And she was getting along so beautifully. I felt good. I was proud of her and grateful for the moment. It was a most valuable moment stretched out for me to appreciate.

I saw the Stick Lady often on the skywalk or out on the sidewalk when the weather was nice. She wasn't always smiling, but I never caught her scowling. After a while, I noticed she had large shoulders making up for the two legs in braces. Her legs were matchsticks just like Russian's.

Beauty is in the eye of the beholder; to me she was beautiful. There was some unstruck harmony, far down inside of me, that her presence had touched, and my music was forthcoming. It lifted me, and I liked it. How was I feeling? I knew this time. I was elated!

This experience altered my understanding of patience, for it had blown out all the proportions and dimensions of patience as I understood it. I peered into this spiritual explosion and waited to see what would come into focus. What appeared was like a dream.

Our group—my friends from both hospitals—and I are carefully making our way along a mountain path in wheelchairs, on Canadian sticks, crutches, canes and with limps. We share this pilgrimage together. Suddenly, coming over a rise, we come upon a deep blue mountain lake sparkling below us in the early morning sunshine.

The wind sweeping through the pines is hushed, and we all instinctively lean slightly forward, listening intently, heads turning to catch the sound. We encounter harmony both within ourselves and with the beauty before us. Drawing in deeply the crisp, clean air, smiles show the vigor expanding within each of us as we recognize the truth in what we behold. Immediately, we are all uplifted by the power of the beauty and splendor. The burden carried by each of us is gone, removed, giving way to a lightness of body and spirit. All of us know the tingle of life coming from an outside force, releasing us so we can transcend our pain and suffering. We are free.

Finally, a soaring red-tailed hawk, wheeling above the lake and banking to catch the next updraft, screams back confirmation of our true primeval reality.

A fantasy enjoyed. Before long, the Stick Lady was to show me that my fantasy and my reality were not all that far apart. This real event came in the midst of my darkness brought on by the divorce. I was about as far down as I had ever been in feeling separated from my family. It is called abandonment. On what appeared to be a miserably bleak day, I found myself in a dubious setting.

I was waiting for a bus to take me home from work. I couldn't afford to drive all the time any more, and besides, I was worn out from doing all the driving. It was my first day riding the bus. Traveling by this new schedule, there was only one express bus home for me. Home was thirteen miles away. If I missed the express, I would have to hike about ten blocks to catch a puddle-jumper some sixty minutes later. It would take me an hour longer to get home and included a ten-minute transfer. I had a great desire to go by the express.

Standing there that day, I was consumed by self-pity over my emotional bankruptcy in the marriage disaster. I felt very much alone in the crowd at the bus stop. I was growing more apprehensive about catching the bus; I was beginning to suspect I had missed it. I knew I was lonely in the crowd. Perhaps it was because I had been neglecting my prayers. I hadn't wanted to pray.

Maybe I even liked wallowing in self-pity, but I could hardly admit that to myself. What would my pride say? I didn't want to look into the full-length mirror of honesty. I certainly wasn't using my tools of recovery, such as reading the Twelve Steps or saying the Serenity Prayer as the Program suggested. Even several telephone calls during the week from concerned group members hadn't turned me in the right direction for help and serenity and vision.

Actually, it was a nice spring day; some blue sky was even showing overhead. Across the street was a new parking lot that had just been blacktopped. Some small trees had been planted in the parking area near the street. But I hadn't noticed any of this. Usually I noticed birds and shrubs and trees and nature. I enjoyed birding, a revival from my childhood, but this day I wasn't in a mood to appreciate nature at all. I was stuck at the self-pity level with probably a few other things thrown in that I couldn't begin to identify.

As I looked up the street in the direction my bus was supposed to come from, I discovered the Stick Lady making her way down the sidewalk on the other side. I studied her from my side of the street and thought of Russian, not so much because she had sticks like his for legs, but because of her gait. Each time she stuck both those Canadian sticks out with her rhythmic movement, her shoulders shot back with the jolt of her body coming down on them. Then came the swing of her dead legs with the force of her entire body coming down on them. Her body was landing on her hip sockets with nothing to take up the shock, no ankles or knees or even toes to cushion the stress. Crash. And crash. Always one more crash.

I could see she wore no scowl. She was looking around as she came along, noticing people passing by and the cars moving up the street. I found myself wondering how far this patient woman had come as she passed by on the other side of the street. And then she did a beautiful thing. She spied those new little trees near the street by the parking lot, and she went closer to inspect them. She stopped, reached up and pulled down a branch to smell a blossom on it. It was a little crab apple tree, and it did indeed have a blossom on it. I knew right away this was a God event. I simply knew it. She, in her simplicity, was showing me on her sticks what I needed to know. The beauty was right there, and she had taken the time to enjoy it. I didn't know how long it had taken her to go just one block, but she had the time to stop and smell the blossom. She showed me that the truly important things in life are so simple and so free. What was it I had said the first time I had seen her? "There, but for the grace of God, go I"?

Now it was, "Here is the grace of God, and it is beautiful as well as free." Here was a mountain lake right in the middle of the busy, asphalt-covered downtown.

I knew God wasn't going to let me stay in my self-pity bag. I knew the dead stuff was finished, and I found myself smiling. I was a cripple no longer. It truly was a sunny day.

"Thank you, God," I said to myself as my bus came up. I knew I was going a new way. It was nice letting someone else do the driving.

"Thank you, God, for always giving me another chance. Riding with you is the best plan. Thanks to you, I made it."

Robert F. Hall was born in Omaha on November 2, 1926, and grew up in Nebraska knowing the meaning of depression and drought. He learned to appreciate nature. His father taught him to fish and hunt and how to camp in the wilderness; his mother showed him the world of art. Birds were an early interest (his grandmother's touch). He has spent his adult life as a priest in the Episcopal Church and in the stock and bond business. Writing is a new pleasure for him.